CHRISTINE E. GUDORF

VICTIMIZATION

Examining Christian Complicity

D1452492

Trinity Press International   Philadelphia

FIRST EDITION 1992

Trinity Press International
3725 Chestnut Street
Philadelphia, PA 19104

Cover design by Jim Gerhard

Library of Congress Cataloging-in-Publication Data

Gudorf, Christine E.
    Victimization : examining Christian complicity / Christine E.
Gudorf.—1st ed.
      p.   cm.
    Includes bibliographical references.
    ISBN 1-56338-044-7 : $13.95 (alk. paper)
    1. Sociology, Christian.   2. Christianity and justice.   3. Church
work with the poor.   4. Liberalism (Religion)—Controversial
literature.   5. Victims.   I. Title.
BT738.G773   1992
261.8—dc20   92-13671
                                                 CIP

This book is printed on acid-free paper.

Printed in the United States of America.

96 95 94 93 92   5 4 3 2 1

CONTENTS

INTRODUCTION

At a recent national meeting of theologians a friend of mine corrected a speaker who had just given a paper on AIDS in which he referred to "AIDS victims." She informed him that organizations of AIDS patients have professed a decided preference for being called "persons with AIDS" (PWAs), that they don't like being defined in terms of their illness. She was right, of course, and so are the PWAs. But one response to her correction muttered by a nearby colleague caught my ear: "Yeah, everybody's tired of hearing about victims: victims of hunger, victims of homelessness, victims of earthquakes, victims of sexual abuse, victims of torture."

Unfortunately, though we do get tired of constant and unending calls for compassion, monetary support, and voluntary requests (most of them phoned in, as if on cue, in the middle of the evening meal), the existence of victims is very real. Precisely because victims are both real and numerous, Christians, as people called to love of neighbor, must exercise some discrimination in approaching victims and victimization. We all want to feel that our concern and efforts on behalf of victims accomplish some reduction in victimization, that at least in some distant future the parade of victims will dwindle and perhaps even cease. If that is to ever occur, we need to not only deal with the present wave of victims, but spend some of our efforts in stemming the forces which create new tides of victims. This, of course, is a massive task, far beyond the ability of this one small book to describe. The task I have set for myself here is to examine some few of the many ways in which Christians and their churches are

1

complicit in the processes which maintain and support victimization. Some of these ways are well known.

Christian faith has been used to legitimate the torture and killing of millions in the Crusades, the conquest of the Americas, the Inquisition, and the programs which preceded the modern Holocaust. Killing, slavery, and torture supposedly legitimized by the gospel have continued in our world, for example in the justification of apartheid in the Dutch Reformed Church of South Africa, or the use of torture and assassination against supposed "godless Communists" by military regimes which call themselves Christian. But there are, of course, also other, more subtle, though no less real or painful, forms of victimization in our world for which those who claim the gospel must take responsibility.

When we look at historic forms of victimization we are often appalled at the failure of victimizers to recognize what atrocities they perpetrate. How, we ask, could the Inquisition, or the conquistadores, really believe that they were saving souls and glorifying God as they burned human beings to death? And yet this is one of the most common aspects of victimization: the extent to which victimizers are unconscious of the evil they do. This lack of consciousness is seldom total, of course, and is often deliberately cultivated. Many of the religious rationales for victimization are just that—not the initiating cause of victimization, but carefully constructed defenses for continuing practices that benefit limited social groups at the expense of others. Ignorance of our common humanity is not random, but chosen and maintained through avoiding all that might lead us to identification with victims: physical proximity, common terms of address and description, shared institutions, knowledge of the other, and recognition of the injustice and unmerited and involuntary suffering present in our world.

But even more appalling and mystifying to most of us who examine the processes of victimization is the extent to which victims themselves become resigned to, accept, and even perpetuate the very victimization that oppresses them. What makes this acceptance worse than the largely unconscious cruelty of victimizers is not any greater moral guilt or responsibility of victims; the victims operate with far less freedom, and therefore far less responsibility, for whatever actions they take within the situation of victimization. What makes their resignation seem worse to us is that once we recognize their resignation we understand that the structure of victimization is much more difficult to destroy than we previously realized: the structure is so powerful that its very victims have been sucked into supporting the evil which oppresses them. For the naive, which includes most of us, it is a shock to understand that there are not just a few "bad guys" out there, and lots of victims waiting for a leader to organize them against their oppressors. Victimization is much more complex than that, as we will see in later chapters. The first major task in liberating victims is to help victims both see themselves as victims and accept that their liberation is possible.

It is obviously in the interests of victimizers that victims internalize their victimization in ways that make them accept their situation. Such acceptance makes it much easier for victimizers to remain blind to the evil they do. It is in this task of supporting victims' internalization of oppression that religion is so useful to victimizers. Religious rationales for victimization not only quell stirrings of conscience among victimizers, but they also mask victimization from those who merely observe from a distance, as well as encourage victims to accept their situation as just, divinely willed, or at least inevitable.

In our society we must struggle to make clear that acceptance of victimization by victims does not eliminate injustice, but only hides it. This is not always clear. For example, one frequent objection to instituting and publicizing a sexual-harassment policy in many universities and companies is that it will produce a rash of sexual-harassment complaints. That is, behavior that has always been accepted, even if deplored, by employees will now be understood as unacceptable, and become the basis of grievances. As one administrator put it, "Making a policy creates victims." But the fact is that there were victims of sexual-harassment all along, even when that victimization was not recognized as such by either the victim or the victimizer. Such an argument would imply that persons tortured by others are not victims unless torture is formally outlawed.

This book will focus on some of the ways that the Christian gospel is used to mask and thereby maintain ongoing victimization in our world. Chapter 1 argues that the uncritical use of scripture as revelatory and authoritative, even among many committed to the liberation of victims, is dishonest and contributes to maintaining victimization in that it invites acceptance of counterliberatory messages in scripture. Chapter 2 suggests that Christians have misinterpreted the gospel regarding the preferential option for the poor by understanding the poor and other victims as recipients of the liberative sacrifices of the non-poor. In fact, the poor and other victims are saved neither by their victimization nor by the liberatory efforts of others, but primarily by their *own* preferential option for the liberation of the poor, which is *more* demanding of them than of the non-poor.

Chapter 3 examines the psychological mechanics of victim-blaming, and in particular the impulse toward victim-blaming in Christian treatment of prudence in redressing social injustice. Romanticization of victims is the focus of Chapter 4, in which I argue that the tendency to romanticize victims both undermines attempts at liberation, and results from a perverse fascination with the cross that distorts human experience. And finally, in Chapter 5 I suggest that the responsibility of the Christian churches for victimization in the area of sexuality runs much deeper than blindness toward and complicity in sexual abuse. Christian teaching—and the lack of teaching—create their own forms of victimization, of which both victims and victimizers are largely unconscious.

CHAPTER 1

SCRIPTURE AND VICTIMIZATION

There is general agreement among Christians that love of neighbor is a Christian imperative, and that first priority among neighbors belongs to those most in need. Though there have been great debates over whether our actions in love of neighbor finally have salvific power, and are debates today over whether orthopraxis or orthodoxy is more central to Christianity, virtually all Christians acknowledge that we are called to act on behalf of our neighbors, especially those most in need.

Needy persons are commonly understood as victims, not necessarily victims of other persons, as in victims of crime, or torture, or political repression, or other forms of physical abuse, but also victims of circumstances, such as sickness, disability, floods, fires, droughts, and hurricanes. We also use the term victim to describe those who suffer from hunger, homelessness, and unemployment, though even among Christians there is recurrent debate about whether these persons are true victims of circumstances beyond their control, or whether they contributed in whole or part to their suffering.

If we ask Christians why they are to act on behalf of victims, the inevitable answer is that scripture says so. They may point to one or more of a hundred different stories or sayings from scripture which urge love of, or service toward our neighbors, or perhaps to the overall example of Jesus of Nazareth in the Gospels.

It is true that in both Hebrew scriptures and Christian New Testament we find stories and sayings demonstrating God's priority for victims, beginning with the liberation of the Hebrew slaves in Egypt, and extending through Jesus' actions on behalf of those who are blind, or lame, people with leprosy, the woman about to be stoned, and the despised poor of his society. In both the prophets and the Gospels we find denunciations of some of the methods of victimization, especially the use of power or wealth to rob the lowly of their rights, property, and dignity. And we find again and again, from both God in Hebrew scriptures and Jesus in the Gospels, the command that we accept as our own God's priority for needy victims.

The message of scripture to all needy victims is understood to be clear and powerful: your situation is not God's intent, but rather offends God, who awaits only human cooperation to liberate you. Scripture therefore can open needy people to awareness of God's love, to their own dignity and self-worth, and to hope for and commitment to a better world for them and their children.[1] In this way, then, scripture can support a theological ethic of liberating victims.

What could be more useful for a praxis (liberating activity) and ethics (critical reflection on praxis) aimed at the relief of victims than finding that a cornerstone of one's religious tradition—scripture— supports such a praxis and ethics? But is scripture really so useful to a praxis and ethics aimed at liberating victims? It seems to me that the traditional reverence for scripture and the contemporary usefulness of scripture as a support for the Latin American campaign against poverty have temporarily blinded many to the ambiguity of scripture, and to the ultimately dangerous antiliberative potential of basing any victim-liberating praxis or ethics on the authority of scripture.

POPULAR ATTITUDES TOWARD SCRIPTURE

When theologians, ethicists, and scripture scholars quote from or refer to scripture, they are understood to be invoking authority. Among Christians, sermons do not always deal exclusively with scripture; sermons may include quotations from or references to current events, classical novels, statements of church or state officials. Such references are regarded as valuable in providing new perspectives, opening new connections to other persons, situations or ideas. But this is *not* how scriptural quotations are understood. The Bible and all its parts are popularly assumed to be true in all senses; the Bible is the basic teaching tool in Christian churches because it is assumed that every passage, however seemingly, obscure, contains divine truth to be mined either literally or figuratively.

Some people have sufficient scriptural training to know that this assumption is not true—that parts of scripture contradict each other, or are ambiguous, or are stridently counterliberatory, and even obscure what we believe to be the central gospel message. But we never-theless invoke scriptural quotations or references in our theological arguments without disavowing the weighty authority popularly accorded scripture. And when we invoke scripture thusly, we utilize this popular understanding of scripture to persuade ordinary Christians to our point of view. Virtually all of us manipulate our readers and hearers in our use of scripture, not consciously, but through our failure to clarify when and how scripture is authoritative. Christian theologians and ethicists in general have been taught the necessity of supporting our arguments with scripture quotations or references regardless of our topic. If there is no apt scriptural quotation, we explain how scripture texts on other subjects indirectly support our argument. This is standard practice. The only common exception is ethicists who oppose fairly consistent scriptural positions on issues such as homosexuality.[2] The task of these writers—to construct a theological/ethical position in opposition to the dominant scriptural position—is made much more difficult by the failure of the rest of theologians and ethicists to be honest about the ambiguity of scrip-ture. It is not only true that the *devil* can quote scripture—and even write it; persons with good motives and poor judgment, such as you and I, often do the devil's work when we quote scripture.

MANIPULATION THROUGH SCRIPTURE

For when we quote without disavowing the traditional authority of scripture, we not only persuade our reader to share our conclusions by bringing them to appreciate the relevance of our text to contemporary life and decisions, but we also reinforce popular attitudes about scriptural authority and infallibility. The future implications of such use of scripture are unsettling and dangerous. Especially when we address victimized groups—the poor, battered women, refugees, racial minorities—with inspiring messages from scripture about liberation, we may be setting them up for exploitations. For we in effect say: you are valuable, God is your protector who loves you *because it says so in scripture.* They are then unprepared to resist as true and authoritative other messages from scripture used by other preachers, teachers, and writers, even if those messages require subordination and resignation to injustice.

Imagine for a moment the effect of the story of Abraham's sacrifice of Isaac on a child victim of paternal abuse.[3] We can preach forever that the message of the story is Abraham's faithfulness to God, but that is not the message that comes through to the child. We can stress that God spared Isaac, but that too is beside the point to the child. The message of the story to the abused child is that God can demand, and has demanded that a father kill his child, and that the good father *agrees* to such a demand. What effect could this have other than terror, and a lingering lack of trust in the love and concern of both God and parents? How can the child, in the face of such a story, see his or her own abuse by a parent as sinful, or expect to find comfort and protection from others, including God? For all the child knows, perhaps the parent is receiving a similar command from God. The most direct and repeated imperative to children in both the Hebrew scriptures and the Christian New Testament is to honor and obey their parents. Children are not told to honor and obey good parents, but all parents; there is no guideline for children to use in determining if there are situations in which obedience is not appropriate.

Similarly, imagine the effect on the millions of battered wives of the opening lines of the household codes of the New Testament: "Wives, be subject to your husbands as you are to the Lord" (Eph. 5:22). Over the last few decades we have accumulated a great deal of research literature on the phenomenon of wife-battering, and the literature is not complimentary to the churches. Women have failed again and again to receive not only substantive help, but even moral support, from their pastors and congregations, and have often been blamed for their own abuse.[4] It is true that much of the message to battered women has been based on misunderstandings of scripture; "Blessed are the meek" (Matt. 5:5a) and "Blessed are the poor in spirit" (Matt. 5:3a), for example, have been interpreted to mean that wives should be meek and poor in spirit in response to abuse, so that they would "inherit the earth" (Matt 5:5b) and to make true that "theirs is the kingdom of heaven" (Matt 5:3b). But explaining that the beatitudes were given in a present sense, that those addressed are blessed *now* because the kingdom which liberates all is at hand and that discipleship means combatting sinful victimization, does not remove from scripture the potential to set the conditions for, excuse, or even demand, the victimization of women. There are many, many stories, and more than a few direct commands, which deny women dignity and personhood and cannot be explained away by claims of poor exegesis.

A last example of scriptural support for victimization in specific situations could be to imagine the effect of Romans 13:1a "Let every person be subject to the governing authorities" or Titus 3:1a "Remind them to be subject to rulers and authorities" on Salvadorean peasants jailed and tortured for participating in literacy drives, or agricultural co-operatives, or human-rights marches, or on the black Christians of the South who risked their lives in the civil rights campaign, or on German Christians who conspired against Hitler. For those among these groups who understand the Bible as authoritative, as divine Word, how can they avoid feelings of divine betrayal, of abandonment? And how many more would have joined them in their work for justice had they not been reminded of these passages and similar scriptural messages?

Among liberal Christians, a standard criticism of conservative fundamentalist preachers and churches is that they use scriptural proof-texting, taking pieces of scripture out of context even when that use distorts the overall message. But liberals are, I believe, guilty of the same distortion, the same selectivity in scripture. While conservative fundamentalists quote, for example, the household codes or Eve's punishment for the Fall to justify women's subordination, many liberals, even some feminists, build their scriptural case for women's equality on equally selective pieces, such as Galatians 3:28 ("There is no longer Jew or Greek, there is no longer slave or free, there is no longer male and female . . ."), or the first creation narrative in Genesis (Gen: 1:1–2:4a). Contrary to liberal assumptions, putting scriptural quotations "in context" does not explain away all the antiliberatory messages of scripture or justify basing the liberation of victims on the authority of scripture. Neither exegesis nor hermeneutics can rescue the moral authority of all scriptural texts. Understanding how scriptural writers came to take positions which can support victimization does not restore to their writings any legitimacy or authority.

In Romans 1:26–27 Paul, in reviewing the wickedness and ungodliness of pagans, says:

> For this reason God gave them up to degrading passions. Their women exchanged natural intercourse for unnatural, and in the same way also the men, giving up natural intercourse with women, were consumed with passion for one another. Men committing shameless acts with men and received in their own persons the due penalty for their error.

We can point out that Paul assumed that God made heterosexual orientation (sexual attraction to the other sex) inherent in all, and did not know, as we do, that for some persons a predominant or even exclusive homosexual orientation is not chosen, but is present at least from early childhood. For such persons, sexual activity with a member of the same sex if not contrary to natural inclination, but in accord with it. Yet our recognition of Paul's limitation does not change Paul's condemnation of homosexual acts themselves, a condemnation which gives support to those who advocate adding to the social hate and discrimination against homosexuals by excluding them from the Christian community.

We do victims of all types no favor by encouraging uncritical approaches to scripture. In fact, we often encourage not only an uncritical dependence on scripture which can be turned against the needy, but also an uncritical dependence upon churches and church authorities, who are understood as the caretakers of, and embodiment of, scriptural truth, rather than as struggling human caretakers of the Christian community.

GIRARD ON VICTIMIZATION AND RELIGION

One of the more interesting critics of religion around issues of victimization is René Girard, French social literary critic. Girard suggests in his *Violence and the Sacred*[5] that scripture, like Greek tragedies and much of ancient mythology, masks how violence functions in human societies. Girard asserts that primitive peoples worshiped violence as sacred, and found it so fascinating that they were easily drawn into escalating spirals of violence of two types: the localized form of the blood feud, and the more general chaos of cultural disintegration that Girard calls the sacrificial crisis. Girard understands the chief function of early religion to have been safeguarding the community from contagion by violence. Religion accomplished this function by providing and legitimizing a ritual sacrifice of a surrogate victim in order to appease the violent appetites of the community without incurring further social violence. The victim had to be a surrogate who could represent the entire community as scapegoat, without being so closely identified with any one part of the community as to necessitate retaliatory violence for the victim's death. Animal sacrifice was the most common form of sacrifice, but human sacrifice was practiced much more often than previously thought, and is the most transparent to us.

According to Girard, this function of religion—providing surrogate victims for sacrifice in order to procure community peace—was lost when states developed independent judiciaries, which could pursue and punish the guilty, without fear of provoking retaliatory blood feuds. Until that time, communities could not focus on the guilt of the offender, for fear of spiraling violence led them to concentrate on appeasing the desire for blood on the part of the victim's family in ways which prevented an outbreak of violence. The early function of religion, says Girard, lives on in Christianity in that its central myth, of Jesus as surrogate victim, tells the tale of collective, unpremeditated murder of a scapegoat, from a perspective which obscures human affinity for violence and instead focuses on God as sending Jesus to die and then raising him.

In *Job: The Victim of His People*[6] Girard argues that Job was chosen as sacrificial victim by his community, and that Job is remarkable only in that he, unlike other victim-heroes, did not accept his role, and is heard to rather consistently reject it even while he consistently agrees with his prosecutors in identifying God with the community who condemns him. Job's refusal to accept the role of surrogate victim prevents the unanimous violence of the community against him from creating the peace and stability intended by the sacrificial victim ritual. Job refuses to "curse God and die" and continues to insist that he is both just and faithful.

There are a number of points at which Girard's work needs to be taken seriously by any student of scripture. One concerns the nature of God in scripture. Girard's understanding of violence as sacred for primitive people is not that different from many previous suggestions that primitive peoples worshiped power—any force they could not control. Violence is power at its starkest. There is no question but that the power of God, understood largely in terms of God's potential for violence, is a chief characteristic recognized and worshiped by the Hebrews and early Israelites.

Furthermore, there are in the Hebrew scriptures a multitude of stories which parallel Girard's argument that human beings are fascinated by violence and therefore need communal actions to stop the natural escalation of violence. The taboos around blood and menstrual blood present in the Mosaic law have, according to Girard, the purpose of containing the violence that blood represents. The warrior returning from the battlefield requires a ritual cleansing from the carnage lest he contaminate the community with violence: thus the oath Jepthah takes to sacrifice the first living thing to greet him upon his return from battle. His daughter has nothing to do with the violence of battle—her very distance, and her importance to him as his only child, made her the perfect victim whose sacrifice would effectively remove from the community all impulses to violence. The whole institution of sacrificial victim worked as a kind of reminder to society that if blood begets blood continuously, then eventually the carnage will proceed until even those farthest away—like Jepthah's daughter—are killed. It is as if the death of that outsider to the violence is the symbol of the death of the whole community, after which there is no one left to kill. The surrogate is a shortcut to the end of the violence, a short cut which bypasses the deaths of the rest of the community which would otherwise have been drawn in.

At one level, Girard is correct to imply that Jesus Christ is another of the surrogate victim-heroes. Jesus Christ is understood to have broken the cycle of death, to have taken on all human sins and sufferings, and to have died for us, thereby saving us. There is a real sense in which centuries of Christians have, ironically enough, lined up with Caiaphas in agreeing that it is expedient that one person die for the many (John 18:14).

Clearly Girard's primary suggestion agrees with the thrust of this book: that human beings need to take responsibility for their own actions, in particular their violent actions against others, rather than continuing to attribute this violence to God and God's will, as was often the case in the Hebrew scriptures. People need to face their own violence not only so that they learn to act more responsibly in the future, but also so that the violence is purged from our conceptions of God.

There are at least three serious questions raised by Girard's work which are not answered in either *Violence and the Sacred* or *Job: Victim of His Friends*. The first is how similar we are to ancient people, specifically, are our communities still threatened by our fascination with violence? The second concerns contemporary society, which seems not only steeped in, but dedicated to the very lack of differentiation which Girard proposes as initiating sacrificial crises in primitive societies. Where is Girard's practical, religious concern for the crisis today? René Girard appreciates that the process of social disintegration is sufficiently advanced in our society to allow us insight into how that process functions. But certainly in the matter of violence and social disintegration Marx's point was well made, "The philosophers have only *interpreted* the world, in various ways; the point, however, is to *change* it."[7] Third, and most crucial, does Christianity, as Girard implies, represent the acceptance and proclamation of the message that the preservation of life and community depends upon the community violently turning on and killing one of its own?

The first question is essentially psychoanalytic. Girard acknowledges frequently that the ritual sacrifice in primitive society was only able to end the social crisis because the people did not understand the process—the substitution—in which they were involved. They did not even understand themselves as dealing with their own violence, for they perceived the divine at work both demanding the sacrifice, and creating human cooperation in the killing of the victim. Since the human community did not see the call for sacrifice as its own, it did not need to face its own proclivity for violence. The question for us today is whether facing our own propensity for violence gives us any greater control over it. We should be careful of any too quick affirmatives here. Surely if modern human beings have not faced our own proclivity to violence in the nuclear arms race, which is still starving almost half the world despite the collapse of one of the two offensive blocs, there is nothing which can make us face it. Is it possible that it is not just violence itself which is attractive, but that human beings are also attracted to collective action, as in what is called the "mob" phenomenon, in which individuals shed their differentiation and act in full accord? Such collective action frequently but not always takes shape in violence. But under the right conditions, a team of well practiced players can sometimes perform "automatically" without apparent thought or will; an audience mesmerized by an enthusiastic preacher can respond as a single entity to the preacher's every command, or a rowdy group of drunks can come to rigid attention to sing their national anthem. If this is a separate phenomenon, then in the cult of sacrificial victims we have two dangerous human appetites together: for violence and for unanimous, undifferentiated, collective action.

The second question suggests that the primary response to Girard's proposal should be religious, that is, practical: what should be done if this is, indeed, how human communities work? Yet this response is absent from Girard, who seems to present social science as replacing the role of religion in primitive societies. But while social science may have inherited religion's interpretative, evaluative role, it has not accepted the practical, conservative task of religion. Girard describes primitive religion as seeking to preserve society from drowning in an orgy of violent blood-letting, by introducing the surrogate victim whose death would end the violence. Primitive religion's interpretative and evaluative roles were largely deceits, camouflage for religion's practical role in conserving society by ending violence through violence. Social science can penetrate the camouflage religion used to screen its secret conservative measures. But if it is to be to modern society what religion was to primitive society, it must take on the more crucial, and active, role of social conservator. Human society is not yet saved.

This takes us to the third question: how does Christianity compare to the primitive religious ritual of the sacrifice of the surrogate victim? A first response by an honest Christian is likely to be "Too closely for comfort!" In fact, what Girard does is to raise, in much more developed and telling fashion, the familiar criticism that Christianity is a religion for slaves. Girard's implication is that Christianity, by ritualizing and calling for imitation of the death and resurrection of Jesus Christ, is structuring and preserving a social situation in which communities regularly purge themselves of violence by choosing a victim to be violently sacrificed. Christians are those who agree to be the victims.

But does the call to imitate Jesus Christ really commit us to the perpetuation of the social cycle of victimization? Is violence an innate urge in human beings, or should human infatuation with violence be interpreted differently? What if violence is not an innate urge, but a response to treatment not befitting humanity? If violence is not like the bad humors that premodern medicine believed built up in the blood and must be purged by bleeding, but rather can be minimized in societies by meeting the various human needs of the inhabitants, then the meaning of the figure of Jesus Christ changes, as does what it means to imitate him. Then the focus is no longer on his death— for it is not his death that saves—but rather on what he did with his *life* even at the risk of death. We are no longer then called to offer our deaths for our community, but to offer our lives to the elimination of the causes of violence. The way in which we understand violence—sin—makes a tremendous difference in the meaning of the good news about Jesus Christ.

Girard gives us a useful perspective from which to examine Christian teaching around the death of Jesus Christ. I suspect that closer examination will demonstrate that a great deal of the Christian tradition on the efficacy of Jesus' death does match Girard's model, in which only violence is seen as able to end violence. What then, do we say to the sacrifice of Jesus, and the other surrogate victims chosen by their societies to satiate blood lust? Can we deny that good came from this evil, if the violence was checked?

Here I think one must challenge Girard. If social violence is not a disease but a symptom of a number of related diseases, then the sacrifice of a surrogate victim serves only to relieve the symptom. The sacrifice is not at all a cure. It does not make the social diseases that produce violence any less dangerous. It only lowers the fever for a minute, an hour, maybe a day. But the fever can return even higher at any time. There is no guarantee.

Or perhaps the institution of sacrificial victims served an even more negative purpose. Perhaps serving up a surrogate victim to satisfy the public's lust for violence functioned not to relieve the public's fever, which may have been caused by bad harvests, corrupt government, or civic disgrace, but to anesthetize the public's brain into forgetting all its woes. That is, perhaps the cult of victims served not to interrupt a cycle of violence, but to further addict the public to violence. The cult served up discrete doses of violence guaranteed to be digestible, and was much safer than the indiscriminate kind of violence to which the public would otherwise have resorted. But violence is violence, and violence is narcotic. A public caught up in violence cannot feel its own pain. It does not know that it is hungry, or tired, or wounded. It has no consciousness to spare for feeling, it only acts until the acting is done, until the public falls apart into its discrete individual persons. Those individual persons can easily become addicted to the experience of surrendering their individual consciousness to the public persona which promises the nirvana of total and unanimous collective action, especially when those individual persons are so pain-ridden and suffering. We can no more know that selecting victims to appease the public's appetite for violence decreased the level of violence in a society than we can know that throwing virgins into smoking volcanoes pacified the angry gods at the core and avoided eruption. Maybe the volcanoes wouldn't have erupted anyway.

Many social critics would undoubtedly suggest that Girard needs to look more closely at revolutionary theory. For to many, the role of religion in serving up victims looks very much like the bread and circuses the ruling Roman elite used to buy off the public, or the modern manipulation of democratic publics into little wars to distract them from bad government or failing economies at home. What is being protected from violence is not necessarily the society itself, but the form of leadership, or more precisely, the leadership elite. The contagious nature of violence is not the only consideration to be made when investigating the institution of sacrificial victims. Also important is the tendency of power structures to maintain themselves by manipulating the masses.

NECESSITY OF CHALLENGING SCRIPTURE

In an ethics centered on the praxis of liberating victims, the traditional authority of scripture must be challenged and disavowed. The necessity of challenging the authority of scripture does not imply that we cannot find truth within scripture, only that we cannot assume that any scriptural text is true and authoritative merely because it is a part of scripture. The recognition that some parts of scripture are counterrevelatory—that they impede the recognition of victimization and efforts toward liberation of victims that are central to God's wishes for human beings—must affect the way we approach scripture as a whole. The revelatory authority of each text must be evaluated and judged in the light of our particular praxis. It is the demands of praxis which determine what is true and authoritative within the entire scriptural canon we inherit from the early church. We must ask: How adequate is this text for the liberation of victims—for the defeat of the unjust social structures that oppress victims, for their spiritual and psychological healing, and for victims' resistance to the sin of complicity in their own victimization? Because praxis shifts historically as new forms of victimization are recognized, what is authoritative within the canon will also undergo some change.

At a practical level we all know that not all parts of scripture are equally revelatory. There is no Christian community which abides by the entire teachings of scripture. Few Christians follow the decision of the Council of Jerusalem in Acts 15:29, forbidding the Gentile Christians to eat blood (strangled meat), a decision based on the Jewish practice of draining the blood from slaughtered animals. Much less do Christians abide by the many commandments of the Mosaic law. We do not stone to death our "stubborn and rebellious" sons (Deut. 21:18–21), we wear clothes of different materials (Lev. 19:19), we do not execute adulterers (Lev. 20:10), and our churches and homes are filled with "graven images" of Jesus, the apostles, and even God, despite the ban on them in Leviticus 26:1. My own Catholic church seems to have deliberately ignored Matthew 23:9 "Call no one your father on earth, for you have one Father—the one in heaven" when it adopted "Father" for addressing priests, as well as 1 Timothy 3:2 and Titus 1:6 when it prohibited married bishops. Reason and consistency demand that we acknowledge that we have set these commands aside, relegated them to the category of the unimportant and irrelevant within scripture. In so doing we have used some criteria other than scripture itself for determining what is revelatory. We cannot claim that we have set these parts aside out of reverence for other parts of scripture, for there had to be some outside criteria used for deciding which parts of scripture were of continuing revelatory force and which were not. We need to be clear that it is our experience of concrete praxis within the Christian community which alerts us to the fact that the perspective from which parts of scripture are written is not liberative, but is at times even antiliberative, and that sometimes we must reconstruct the liberative story from the biblical materials furnished by the powers and principalities. The text is not always the truth, but only one source for determining the truth through a process of interpretation beginning with the concrete demands of praxis. The authority of any particular passage rests with its ability to speak to or express our individual and collective experiences of liberation, growth, and the presence of the divine, and not from the fact that it is a part of the Holy Bible venerated by Christians for almost two thousand years. We must remember that Jesus demanded of his apostles that they have faith in him not based on signs (such as the survival and spread of Christianity over 2000 years) but because his message and actions accorded with their most deeply felt aspirations and needs, and satisfied their yearning for divine presence and love.

SCRIPTURAL ADEQUACY: THE CASE OF INCEST

Let us look for a moment at the testimony of those who work with female child victims of incest,[8] and at the inadequacy they perceive in scripturally-based theological treatment of incest. There can be little doubt that children who experience incest are victims in the fullest sense. Because they are children they are largely powerless against adults, especially against close adult relatives, and many of them suffer lifelong agony as the result of incest. Contemporary research finds that incest victims, the average age of whose first incestuous incident is 11.1 years, suffer traumatic sexualization, and feelings of stigmatization, betrayal, and powerlessness. These four trauma-causing factors activate "negative self images. Victims see themselves as weak, helpless, needy, frightened and out of control."[9] They thus need to restore damaged self-images, as well as to learn to cope with a world in which such events occur. Most do not receive much help in these two tasks. Incest is understood to be even more underreported than rape: Diana E. H. Russell reports that in her study only 5 percent of child sexual abuse and 2 percent of child incest cases were reported.[10]

This lack of help is assumed to be one major cause for the revictimization of incest victims: 82 percent of incest victims are later victims of serious sexual assault by nonrelatives, compared to 48 percent of those who have not been incestuously abused. Close to three times as many incest victims as those never victimized by incest report having been raped in marriage. Over twice as many incest victims as nonvictims of incest report physical violence toward them in marriage.[11] A common effect of incest is "that their self-esteem may be so damaged that they [the victims] don't think they deserve their own loving self-protection, which can result in repeated revictimizations, each one of which can undermine a woman's self-esteem further."[12] Incest victims demonstrate high levels of alcohol and drug abuse, lack of trust in others, high suicide rates, and difficulty in forming adult relationships compared to nonvictims.[13]

What does scripture have to say about incest? Very little. The most direct passage is from the Mosaic law on incest taboos. Leviticus 18:6–18 gives a long list of relatives whose nakedness a man is forbidden to uncover (with whom sex is forbidden): his mother, father's wife, sister, grandchildren, aunts by blood or marriage, daughters-in-law, and sisters-in-law. Conspicuously absent is a ban on sex with one's daughter, though we know that 4.5 percent of girls in the United States are victims of father-daughter incest,[14] which is the most traumatic, most damaging, and most coercive form of incest, as well as the form which is most often repeated.[15] We know today that the treatment of incest in the Mosaic law is one aspect of the overall historical understanding of women as property of men; the law functioned to protect the property rights of men from other men. Unbetrothed daughters were the property of the father, and therefore his to use. Therefore while there existed in principle a ban on sex between near kin, there is no specific ban on father-daughter sex.

Another scriptural source on incest is the story of Lot and his daughters who fled their home during God's destruction of Sodom and Gomorrah (Gen. 19:30–38). Lot and his daughters became solitary cave-dwellers, and the daughters came to despair of ever marrying and having children (understanding that their purpose in life was motherhood, and only motherhood could support them later in life). They therefore got their father drunk on two successive nights and lay with him, in order to get pregnant. Genesis records their offspring as Moab and Ben-ammi, the founders of the Moabites and the Ammonites. There is no condemnation of this incest in the story, and more than a subtle hint of praise for their ingenuity and daring. This story is dangerous not only because it fails to condemn incest, but because it focuses on daughter-initiated incest. To grant this story any authority because it is part of the Bible makes it at least implicitly paradigmatic, and thereby suggests that incest may be daughter-initiated. This sets present-day child victims up for victim-blaming.

The dominant New Testament message to children, continued from the Hebrew scriptures, is that children honor and obey their parents (Eph. 6:1 and Col. 3:20). This command is given in absolute form; there is no treatment of situations in which honor and obedience might not be appropriate.

What have we in scripture to use in responding to incest offenders, or to those small but organized groups which argue that incest, and adult/child sexual activity in general is an effective practice of love of neighbor? More importantly, what response do we have in scripture to victims of incest? Scripture is largely silent. What it does say is not helpful and can actually support abuse. Scripture does not recognize incest as a form of victimization. It is only in Christian praxis, in working with those whose experience of incest has induced trauma and led them to revictimization, failed relationships, and self-destructive behavior, that we see incest as serious victimization. Only at this point can we turn to carefully selected passages of scripture which affirm God's ongoing presence, concern, and preferential love for victims.

The centrality of praxis also challenges the authority of scripture in comparison with other theological disciplines, and with other non-theological disciplines which explain human reality. With a center in liberating praxis, the whole of scripture is no longer primary, much less sufficient, as a resource for ethics. The classical seminary model for dividing and implicitly ranking the theological disciplines (in which scripture comes first, then church history, systematics, and ethics) comes under attack when truth is understood as something which unfolds within the work of praxis, not something which was complete in the scriptural past. Scripture is a collection of some of the accounts about Jews and Christians attempting to respond to the call of our God, who continued to interact with human beings after the end of New Testament times. It becomes difficult to explain why scriptural accounts of attempts to respond to the call of the reign of God should be more relevatory than those of black Christians in the civil rights movement or of incest victims in therapy programs or Latin American Christians suffering tyrranical, even genocidal military governments.

Not only does it become difficult to defend the primacy of scripture in the task of theological reflection, but it becomes necessary to ask whether the division of the theological disciplines can be defended at all. Can ethics and scripture, or church history and systematics, really be treated separately? More than this, are the limits of the theological disciplines defensible? If praxis is the central task, then aren't the social sciences—history, economics, sociology, and psychology—equally as important resources as scripture and systematic theology? If love of neighbor, especially the most victimized, is a Christian imperative, then aren't the disciplines and mediums which make us aware of and give us understanding of victimization as essential as church history or scripture for opposing the sin of victimization?

THE PRACTICAL PROBLEM: POPULAR ACCESS TO SCRIPTURE

Even if scripture is neither a sufficient nor an infallible source for grounding a liberating praxis and ethics, one issue remains. Can scripture be useful, even as one of many sources, in reflecting on the liberation of victims? The primary problem is that since the liberation of victims is an imperative for all Christians, any useful source for reflecting on the praxis of liberating victims must be accessible to all. But access to scripture not only requires the ability to *read* scripture; it requires the ability to discern the liberating from the counterliberatory in scripture. How accessible are the liberatory messages of scripture to the general public?

In the Protestant Reformation the Reformers, influenced by the new vernacular translations made available by the invention of the printing press, insisted on the ability of all Christians to read and interpret scripture. In contrast Catholic authorities continued for a time the traditional practice that church authorities teach and interpret scripture which remained in Latin. The Catholic church since Vatican II has stressed to its laity the importance of regular reading and meditation on scripture, and thus popular religious practice today does not differ greatly between Catholics and Protestants. There are specific scriptural texts on which the Catholic church, and many individual Protestant churches, insist on their particular denominational interpretation, but with these exceptions, the assumption is that individuals can adequately, though not perfectly, interpret scripture.

At the same time, scripture scholarship has exploded, becoming incredibly more complex. Scripture scholars now use not only sophisticated linguistic analysis and the insights of archeology, but also comparisons with extra-canonical Jewish and Christian texts and secular texts of the time in interpreting scripture. This has led to major shifts in the interpretation of scripture among the experts. Scripture scholarship has become so complex that it is not uncommon for specialists in particular books of scripture to dismiss the opinions of any not specialized in their text. What possibility does the ordinary Christian have of adequately interpreting all of scripture? Careful attention to the text is not sufficient. For example, the ordinary Christian who defends the Israeli measures against the *intifada* on the grounds that the Lord told the Hebrews to conquer and hold the land, even to slaughtering the inhabitants and enslaving women and children, cannot know of the clear archeological evidence that the Hebrew "conquest" of Palestine was not a major military invasion, but a gradual and peaceful infiltration, that the Israelites lived side by side with Canaanites—which is how the Canaanite religious practices came to be such a temptation to the Israelites. The account of the conquest was composed after the settlement, and was more a wish from hindsight than an account of what happened. The implication of the archeological evidence for the conquest is a tremendously important corrective if we are to use scripture as a source for reflecting on God's will in situations of disputed religious claims over land. But this evidence is largely the exclusive possession of an educated elite. Are our only choices, then, to exclude scripture as a source for ethical reflection on praxis, or to exclude all but scripture scholars from ethical reflection?

In our world today perhaps the most obvious heirs of the Protestant reformers who insisted that the common person could read and interpret scripture are the members of the basic ecclesial communities of Latin America (most of them, interestingly enough, Catholic). They claim the Bible as their book, and as central to their work of liberating the victims of poverty. They have little if any access to scripture scholarship. Yet we now have many translated accounts of their ability to mine scripture for rich insights into their own situation—insights that are not found in academic scriptural interpretation, but which are profoundly moving to Christians even in very different contexts.[16] Their use of scripture is effective in grounding a liberating praxis: a praxis which produces community initiatives in health and education, agricultural co-operatives, and political solidarity. Their lack of access to scripture scholarship does not seem to impede their praxis; many spokespersons for these communities suggest that a better alternative to academic scholarship in interpreting scripture is to approach scripture from the context of praxis, that from such a perspective the ambiguities in scripture yield a liberating thread which runs through scripture despite presence of occasional counterliberatory messages.

Without denying the very real and original insights gleaned from scripture in these Latin American communities, for which we are all indebted, I want to suggest two limitations to this method. Its adequacy is limited both with respect to the type of victimization on which its praxis focuses, and with respect to its potential universalization; that is, it works best for praxis around poverty (rather than sexuality or politics) and is not easily translatable to the First World.

Poverty, the suffering it creates, and the injustice which often causes it, is a common theme in both the Hebrew scriptures and the New Testament. The Latin American poor understand their world much like that of the Gospels, liken themselves to the marginated followers of Jesus and to the farmers, fishermen, and day laborers of the parables. They know venal tax collectors, feel suspicious of the military, and pray for miracles to heal the many debilitating illnesses which afflict them and their children. Thus they are not tempted to read scripture as a history of a "real time" to which they are called to assent, but instead read it as paradigmatic, as an account from which they can learn, which can be of real use in dealing with the present. They do not understand history as linear, always new and progressive; in scripture they look for a relevant social message, not merely the truth about the past or a personal spiritual message.[17] The approach of the Latin American poor to scripture unleashes some compelling messages, which is a major reason for the appeal of liberation theology in the world outside Latin America: scripture comes alive, and is intimately related to the real-life struggles of Christians. For example, reflection in many base Christian communities has long dealt familiarly with the biblical concepts of idols and demons, and has no trouble identifying the idols and demons that plague their lives today. Seeing their own suffering mirrored so openly in the masses of poor people surrounding them, these people in Latin America cannot ignore or suppress their pain, and must seek explanations. Inevitably, many are forced to consider the national security state, official corruption, the reverence for technology, progress and modernity, economic/political dependency, multinational corporations, and the process of accumulation itself, as contenders for the role of idols and demons.

We might be tempted to conclude, then, that scripture is adequately interpreted by the masses at least with regard to poverty. But even this is too simplistic. For it is to ignore the fact that the fastest growing religious movements in Latin America among the poor are not basic ecclesial communities, but rather pentecostal-holiness churches that use a literalist, politically conservative approach to scripture in which personal salvation, and not liberating praxis, is central. To accept the argument that basic ecclesial communities can adequately interpret scripture on poverty is to leave them on their own to deal with a very different use of scripture on poverty by the pentecostal-holiness churches that stress the literalist implications of "my kingdom is not from this world," (John 18:36) "the poor you have always with you," (John 12:8) "Render to Caesar the things that are Caesar's and to God the things that are God's," (Matt. 21:21) as well as Paul's "Let every person be subject to the governing authorities." The very fact that the pentecostal-holiness churches are growing so rapidly among the Latin American poor says something about the ability of these people to interpret scripture for themselves. Without access to scripture scholarship how can they know of the Jewish background of "Render to Caesar;" that first fruits and other taxes were traditionally paid to the Temple as acknowledgment that the land was God's, lent to the Jews for their use. The Romans claimed the land by right of conquest, and demanded taxes as acknowledgment of Caesar's ownership; for a Jew to pay the taxes amounted to renouncing God's ownership of the land, and putting Caesar in God's place. The Temple still collected the taxes, but the religious meaning of the taxes under the Roman conquest changed from reverence for God to rejection of God.[18] This background gives a radical twist to Jesus' "Render to Caesar . . ." How could anyone, solely on the basis of the New Testament story, begin to penetrate the different levels of meaning in this saying? Thus even within the various issues that arise under consideration of the issue of poverty in scripture there is ambiguity in dealing with the text alone, without scriptural scholarship.

There are other issues in scripture around which liberating praxis is even more impossible without the insights offered by the tools of scripture scholarship, which the masses lack. In dealing with sexism in scripture, for example, the perspective from below is limited more or less to noting that individual writers of scripture were influenced by their own social conditioning, and that both the Hebrew scriptures and the New Testament include conflicting treatment of women. Because the popular approach in basic ecclesial communities begins with liberative praxis, it tends to leap to those sections of the Bible useful for praxis and ignore competing messages. What then happens when poor women, who have become excited about and transformed by the biblical messages about the worth of the poor and the reasons for hope, become aware that this same book repeatedly orders women to submit to husbands, treats the giving and taking of women, their rapes and killing, as matters of male perogative? For every Mary who sits at Jesus' feet among the disciples, for every Judith who judges Israel, there are a score of powerless abused women who go nameless and undefended in scripture, in the New Testament as well as the Hebrew scripture.[19]

Without the very sophisticated work of scholars like Elisabeth Schüssler Fiorenza, the communities of praxis will not know that the most sexist parts of the New Testament were the result of a historical movement to marginalize women, slaves, and the poor from their original leadership positions in the Jesus movement.[20] Ignoring the nonliberatory treatment of women in the New Testament prevents recognition of the process by which co-optation and creeping chains get forged even within communities pledged to resisting and overcoming the captivity of sin.

What this suggests is that in certain types of liberating praxis, of which the liberation of victimized women is an example, scripture alone, without access to scripture scholarship, is very limited as a resource. On the other hand, the scriptural scholarship regarding sexism demonstrates very well that the discovery of revelatory force toward liberation in scripture is dependent upon the prior involvement of the interpreter in liberating praxis. The most useful insights for praxis opposing the victimization of women have consistently come not from scripture scholars per se, but from women engaged in praxis who also happened to possess the tools of sophisticated scripture scholarship.

Popular use of scripture for praxis as found in the basic ecclesial communities also encounters difficulties with universalization to other locales. We know from recent research in Brazil that basic ecclesial communities are most advanced—engaged in projects to improve the local infrastructure—among the rural poor and recent urban immigrants. While basic ecclesial communities also exist among the middle class, often due to pastoral plans emerging from the diocesan level, middle class ecclesial communities are more likely to function as mini-parishes, and their social projects tend to be limited to general community service rather than activity with implications for systemic change.[21] This would suggest reservations about the effectiveness of basic ecclesial communities in largely urban, middle class, First World societies.

First World Christians do not experience much similarity between their lives and society and those described in scripture. It takes much deeper digging in scripture for them to find relevance to their lives, and that relevance is most often found at the level of personal relationships and what is regarded as interior spiritual life. First World Christians approach scripture more historically and less mythically than most of the Third World poor. For indigenous Third World culture, written history does not necessarily represent truth and right— their official histories have often been written by their conquerors, and are the history of their subjugation, followed by the deeds of their conquerors. Truth for them does not nearly so much consist of a record of historical events. It is the successful, the conquerors, the prosperous, the powerful, who believe that when we look to factual history we find truth. The Latin American poor tend to look not to the facts of the Bible stories, but the meanings, and in uncovering those meanings they draw on their own realities. Theirs is a functional interest.

Carlos Mesters tells the following story from a Brazilian base community:

> Once, in Goias, we read the passage in the New Testament (Acts 17:19) where an angel of the Lord came and freed the apostles from jail. The pastoral worker asked his people: "Who was the angel?" One of the women present gave this answer: "Oh, I know. When Bishop Dom Pedro Casaldaliga was attacked in his house and the police surrounded it with machine guns, no one could get in or out and no one knew what was going on exactly. So this little girl sneaked in without being seen, got a little message from Dom Pedro, ran to the airport and hitched a ride to Goiana where the bishops were meeting. They got the message, set up a big fuss, and Dom Pedro was set free. So that little girl was the angel of the Lord. And it's really the same sort of thing."[22]

It is almost impossible without extensive training in remytholigization for First World persons to approach scripture in this way. We approach it first as historical truth, and then have to work backward to its original purpose as myth—as stories with messages about ultimate reality. When we read the accounts of the resurrection, we first ask how did Jesus rise from the dead—in what form, what material substance, and how were the laws of nature affected? Among the Latin American poor, there is strongly felt intuition that the Christlike martyrs of the people, of whom Archbishop Oscar Romero is perhaps best known, live resurrected in the struggles of their people. They approach scripture from a particular practical perspective, asking what it has to say about the liberation of victims today. We should not abandon, even if we could, the more critical, speculative perspective bred into us by our cultural history; we cannot undo our past, the effect of the Enlightenment and the scientific revolution, on our consciousness. But perhaps we could learn from these people that criticism and speculation are not valuable in themselves, but only when they serve the praxis of liberating victims. If *we* are to approach scripture as myth aimed at enhancing the praxis of liberation, we need to do so through scriptural scholarship, which can take us back to the mythic perspective from which scripture itself was written.[23]

Where does this leave us? To what extent can scripture be a resource for all Christians in the work of liberating victims? To some extent we shall have to wait and see. But our waiting cannot be passive. The first task is for the churches and all Christians to recognize that scripture itself accepts some forms of victimization, is blind to other forms, and is to some degree ambiguous about many forms. The second task is to accept human experience in general, of which scripture is a part, as the basic source in which we discern God's revelation from the perspective of our involvement in the praxis of liberating victims. This is no small task, and calls for great courage in the churches. We long for security, for certain knowledge of God's will. Christians have tended to feel that discerning present applications of what was regarded as the reliable biblical evidence of God's will in the past is daunting, and perhaps beyond our capabilities. The idea that there is *no* source which lays out in clear, unambiguous terms God's will as expressed in the past tremendously expands the task of discernment, and thereby increases our burden of responsibility. We do not *want* the burden of constantly evaluating the consequences of our actions, the direction of our communities, and the adequacy of our spiritualities as we reflect on our praxis of liberating victims. But there is little choice unless we hide from our own discovery. For once it is clear that scripture can support victimization, we must either critically discern the revelatory from the counterrevelatory in scripture, or understand our God as a God who permits, chooses or desires the existence of victimization.

There are periodic suggestions, usually when some new problem with scripture has arisen (such as the problem of sexist language, for example), that we need to change and edit scripture. We could recon-

sider all of scripture and create a new canon containing only liberatory material. This would require virtually eliminating some books,
and massive editing of many. A daunting task, and a terrible idea.
Liberation is not a static concept. The signers of the Declaration of
Independence and the Constitution understood themselves as liberators, as they were for their own day. But the Fifteenth Amendment
was necessary to rectify their failure to understand the Negro as a
human being. Similarly, the Nineteenth Amendment was necessary
before the Constitution treated women as full citizens. Contemporary
Christians have no reason to believe ourselves exempt from such
moral blindness. A new canon would also be flawed, and it would also
reinforce the dangerous assumption that there can be a religious
source that lays out for us, completely developed, the meaning and
scope of liberation—that we need not consult our experience, our
history, our hearts, that we need not engage in the tremendous task
of discerning God's will.

We would do much better to keep the Bible as is, to teach it as we
teach the Middle Ages, the Reformation, the conquest of the Americas—as evidence that we are and have always been a people who
have both risen to and sunk far below God's desires and expectations
for us, a people who often misinterpreted God's will, and sometimes
cloaked our own half-conscious needs or desires in the divine mantle.

Chapter 2

PREFERENTIAL OPTION: GREATER CHALLENGE TO THE POOR

One of the clearest Christian teachings relevant to the suffering of victims is preferential option for the poor. Though the language of preferential option for the poor is a rather recent addition to theological thought, and developed out of a particular approach to Christian life and theology within Latin American Christianity, the understanding that the poor as suffering victims have a priority in God's concern, and should therefore have a priority for Christians, is not at all recent in Christianity. And yet there is a great deal of debate both within the Christian tradition and within the churches today over both the identity of the preferred poor and the reasons why the poor have priority with God.

God's preferential concern for the poor in scripture is more than an attitude on God's part; salvation history reveals the ongoing activity of God on behalf of the poor. But God's liberating activity on behalf of the poor depends upon the willingness of persons of good will—both poor and non-poor—to cooperate with God in this activity. If the cooperation of human beings is necessary for God's preferential option to be effective, then the churches have an obligation not only to teach that God has a preferential option for the poor. The churches have a further obligation to teach Christians why it is that poverty is an affront to God—a sin—and what it means to cooperate with God in liberating the poor from poverty. In our day, it is clear that the churches have not succeeded in this task, for many Christians either misunderstand the meaning and purpose of preferential option for the poor, or refuse to accept it as central to Christian life.

PREFERENTIAL OPTION VS. TEMPORAL RETRIBUTION

Many Christians dismiss preferential option for the poor out of preference for temporal retribution as divine policy.[1] Temporal retribution is the belief that God rewards and punishes human behavior in this life. Belief in temporal retribution disposes the believer to interpret human suffering and misfortune as divine punishment for transgressing God's commands, and human well-being as reward for obedience to divine command. Preference for temporal retribution as the form God's justice takes in this world is understandable. If behavior is rewarded or punished in this world, then we can know where we stand. We can model ourselves on the successful, and avoid the behavior of those who suffer punishment. We can know how well we please God by looking at our status in the world. Even more, if God's justice is swift and clear so that the innocent are rewarded and only the guilty are punished, then we do not need to fear suffering if we are innocent. We do not need to tremble in the night at all the evils and sufferings which exist in the world—such as abject poverty, epidemics, or tragic accidents—for these will only strike the guilty. People who are relatively comfortable have great incentive to prefer temporal retribution over preferential option for the poor.

There is no doubt that temporal retribution is assumed in many parts of scripture. And yet even in the Hebrew scriptures where themes of temporal retribution are strongest, the events understood as of central revelatory significance in Judaism, and later for Christianity, seem directly to repudiate theories of temporal retribution. Scriptural accounts of the foundation event in Jewish history—God's election of the Hebrews and deliverance of them from slavery in Egypt—carries no hint either that the suffering and enslavement of the Hebrews was God's punishment, or that God's election was due to any merit on the part of the Hebrews. Rather, the election of the Hebrews was understood as evidence of God's compassion for the cries of the suffering. It was Jewish interpretation of their election as based on their merit, or conferring merit on them, which allowed unfounded pride in their riches and achievements, and consequent sin on the part of the Israelites: "Because you have not remembered the days of your youth" (Ezek. 16:43a), "but you have trusted in your beauty" (Ezek. 16:15). Hosea 13:4–6 speaks of how after God cared

for and fed Israel, she became proud of heart and forgot, in her satisfaction, that *God* had saved her. In Hosea 12:7–9 the trader Ephraim
exemplifies this pride and forgetfulness: "in his hands are false bal-
ances, he loves to oppress"—while he congratulates himself on all the
wealth he has gained for himself while committing no offense.

Similarly, in the giving of the Mosaic law which became central to
all later Jewish discourse on God's intentions and on human obligation, the instructions regarding treatment of the poor, slaves,
servants, widows, orphans, and strangers made clear that the
vulnerability or misfortune of these groups were not to be seen as
deserved, but rather that these conditions were to be redressed or
ameliorated precisely because the Israelites were to imitate God who
had intervened to treat the Israelites with compassion (Lev. 25).

The inclusion of the book of Job in the Old Testament also speaks
against the theory of temporal retribution. The central point of the
book is a rejection of temporal retribution and a resulting affirmation
of the existence of innocent suffering, which God's speeches reveal is
rooted in the great gift of freedom which God lovingly conferred on
both human and nonhuman creation. The conclusion of Job is that
real faith—disinterested faith—is possible for human beings only
because there is no temporal retribution.[2]

The pattern of understanding suffering as punishment for sin is
most clearly exemplified in the Old Testament warnings of the prophets. The prophets presented the destruction of Israel and Judah by
surrounding enemies as God's punishment for Jewish apostasy.[3] But
while the prophets presented Israel's enemies as tools used by God
to punish Israel's sin, they also presented conquest by enemies as a
natural result of disobeying the law, which had been designed by God
to create a strong nation bound together by justice. When the people
refused to honor the law, social cohesion lessened, and disintegration
began, thus giving Israel's enemies their chance.[4] Thus, even within
the paradigmatic example of suffering as resulting from sin, the
prophets offered an explanation which did not require God to will this
suffering. A second reason that the prophets are not a sufficient
source for proving temporal retribution is that the prophets describe
Israelite apostasy as exemplified by the oppression of the poor by the
rich in opposition to God's law. But the punishment for apostasy is
visited upon all—in fact social disasters such as war and occupation
take a worse toll on the poor than the non-poor. Thus the Israelite
poor who were the victims of the rich suffer defeat with them—not

an example of just retribution at all. Temporal retribution is not, then, even for the prophets, the sole explanation of suffering.

Within the New Testament, the Gospels are very clear that Jesus never attributed any sin to the hungry whom he fed, the sick he healed, the possessed he exorcised, the dead he raised, or the children, women, and public sinners he defended and treated with respect. Their need was not the result of their sin, and they received cures and forgiveness not because they were virtuous, but because they were needy. "Daughter, your faith has made you well; go in peace, and be healed of your disease" (Mark 5:34). Jesus on more than one occasion directly repudiated temporal retribution. He insisted that the blind young man was not blind due to any sin of his or his parents, that the persons killed by Herod were not the most guilty Galileans, and that those killed by the falling tower in Siloam were no worse sinners than others in Jerusalem (Luke 13:1–5). Jesus' parable of the workers in the vineyard demonstrated that God deals with persons not in terms of temporal retribution, but on the basis of need. All laborers are paid the same full day's wages because they share the same need to eat at the end of the day, regardless of the number of hours worked (Matt. 20:1–16).

In fact, Jesus explained that virtuous behavior—merit—is not the precondition for, but rather the response to, addressing people's needs. When the woman sinner came and washed the feet of Jesus with her tears and dried his feet with her hair, Jesus said to Simon, his host, who wanted to send the woman away, that "her sins, which were many, have been forgiven; hence she has shown great love" (Luke 7:47). When Jesus then told her that her sins were forgiven because of her faith, this was not the original act of forgiving sin, but a confirmation for her of the forgiveness she had felt which prompted her loving action in the first place.

The fact that temporal retribution is so often assumed in scripture stories seems to reflect not so much divine revelation as it does the basic human hunger for justice and order. This hunger for justice often leads human beings to generalize from the fact that sin does often (but not always) cause apparent suffering to the sinner, to assertions that the experience of suffering is the result of sin. The same human desire to believe that a just order prevails allows human beings to be misled by those who desire to attribute to God the suffering their injustice causes others, in order to be acquitted of their own guilt. For example, a recent local news story told of a landlord whom tenants praised for attending the funeral of a three-year-old who fell out of an unscreened, unbarred, fourth-floor window in one of his buildings. The landlord was quoted as saying that only God knew why the innocent child had been called to heaven.

PREFERENTIAL OPTION: WHO ARE THE POOR?

Even among many Christians who accept preferential option for the poor there is great disagreement as to who are the poor God prefers. The two most common choices are for the "poor in spirit," or for the poor as including all the socially marginated, economically deprived, and excluded members of society.

There is a great deal of variety in interpretation of this phrase "poor in spirit."[5] In the face of the Gospel accounts of Jesus' ministry there can be no validity to understanding "poor in spirit" to refer only to those who have accepted their suffering meekly, for this would exclude all those who came to Jesus to ask release from their conditions and to whom Jesus responded with both miraculous relief and praise for the faith which prompted their requests. Jesus' teaching made clear that all were free and encouraged to ask God for relief, for Jesus insisted that God was a loving father who would not give stones to children who asked for bread (Matt. 7:9).

There seems to be a general consensus that the phrase "poor in spirit" refers to an interior openness to the activity of God in one's life and world. This interior openness can be related to the condition of material poverty, since the Gospels make clear that Jesus understood that the poor were more interested in his message about the kingdom because their interests were more neglected in the status quo: they were the sheep without a shepherd for whom he felt compassion (Matt. 9:36). God had revealed the message of the kingdom more clearly to the poor (the "infants" of Matt. 11:25) who responded to the invitation to "Come to me, all you that are weary and carrying heavy burdens, and I will give you rest" (Matt. 11:28).

One way that understanding the preferential option for the poor in terms of the "poor in spirit" has sometimes functioned has been to legitimate the holding of riches by those who claim a lack of attachment to worldly possessions.[6] Emphasis on one's interior disposition rather than on outward disposition was one way of adapting a monastic Christianity for the laity, for whom preferential option for the materially deprived proved difficult to reconcile with the demands of social life.[7] Aquinas' view that Christians were obliged to give their surplus wealth to the poor—surplus wealth being that above and beyond what was necessary to live in accordance with one's station in life—is such an attempt to reconcile social custom with the demands of Jesus. Understanding the poor in terms of nonattachment to possessions allowed the well-to-do to be included among the preferred, and countered the problem posed by Jesus' words concerning the difficulty that the rich face in reaching salvation (Mark 10:23–27).

This approach obviously lends itself to abuse, the most obvious being that it allows Christians to ignore the suffering of those materially deprived in favor of a focus on the interior life. Yet because the materially poor do not exclusively constitute the poor of Jesus, and because the Gospels do give some support for stressing interiority, it cannot be dismissed out of hand. Perhaps the best way to approach it is to accept the stress on interiority while insisting that for Jesus, the test of whether one is attached to worldly possessions comes when one is faced with the materially poor. The demand of Jesus that we prepare for judgment by treating each person in need as we would treat Jesus himself (Matt. 25:31–46) makes clear that the command that we love one another is to be understood in concrete terms of ministering to the needs of others—to their thirst, hunger, homelessness, captivity, and other deprivations. In the face of a needy world, continuing to possess riches while maintaining one has no interior attachment to them becomes extremely suspect.

Yet another approach common among supporters of preferential option for the poor is to interpret the poor as encompassing the powerless, marginalized, and demoralized in addition to the economically deprived. Material poverty is a chief cause of these conditions, but there are certainly others, just as there are types of oppression that *result* in material poverty, such as racial or religious discrimination. Some of those who are poor in this broader sense are the sick, those possessed (mentally ill), and those understood as public sinners, such as homosexuals or drug users are today.

Within the Mosaic law it was recognized that the conditions of some human beings left them defenseless, and that God was the ultimate defender *(go'el)* of these persons. Widows and orphans, the poor, and strangers to the land of Israel were all understood to be under the special protection of Yahweh. Jesus seems to have extended the boundaries of this group in his own preferential option for the poor. This method of accepting preferential option for the poor includes aspects of the "poor in spirit" approach without absolutizing interiority. It recognizes that poverty is a complex phenomenon, neither totally material nor totally psychological. The abandoned inner city child who survives for some years by scavenging garbage and mugging the elderly is not automatically restored to full humanity by the provision of regular food and shelter. Neither is the teenage runaway restored to full humanity when helped to understand that she is not "bad," that her basic problem was an abusive parent in a dysfunctional home. Helped to leave drugs and prostitution, she is still a high school dropout without skills, work, or a supportive family. Material life and psychic life are inseparably bound together for the poor as for all of us. For these reasons we cannot draw, too finely, the limits on who is among the poor, though we will need to clarify greater and lesser degrees of need among the categories of the poor. We must make decisions as to whether we will invest ourselves in structural attempts to redress unemployment, or choose to focus on providing shelter for the homeless, or sanctuary for refugees, or shelters for battered women and children. Will we work against racial discrimination in housing and hiring, or to keep pregnant teens in school, or provide health care for the uninsured? It is often necessary to consider different degrees of need in choosing where to commit ourselves; at other times the decision will be based upon an analysis as to where our own efforts could be most effective.

Understanding the beneficiaries of preferential option as the marginated, powerless, and demoralized as well as the economically deprived seems to both best fit the scriptural evidence and best respond to the objective needs of suffering neighbors.

POLITICAL OPPOSITION TO PREFERENTIAL OPTION

Within the churches, there is not only debate about who are the poor. There is also debate about social applications of preferential option. Many persons understand preferential option for the poor to apply to individual behavior, especially to the private realm of human life, but not to social policy. Such understandings are rooted in a political vision strongly informed by liberal individualism. The division which many Christians insist exists between religion and politics is rooted in their instinctive application of preferential option for the poor within their private lives, while they reject preferential option in socio-economic political policy. For these people, differences between these two aspects of life are crucial. Preferential option for the poor is necessary within the private realm, for it corresponds to the impulses of the heart. It is regarded as natural to give priority to the neediest among one's children, to balance the demands made upon us by parents, spouses, children, friends, and neighbors by responding first to those with the greatest need. We do not need the parables of the prodigal son or the lost coin when one of our children falls ill in order to spur us to give more attention and care to that child than healthy siblings. In popular understanding, there is no real imperative for giving exactly the same care, concern and attention at all times to each within our private realm.

But the impulses of the heart that govern our private lives are not understood as adequate for political decisions, which are thought to be better based on rational calculation. This rational calculation, which undergirds popular political wisdom, is based on a particular understanding of human nature divorced from the assumptions that govern action within the private realm. We assume that the greatest good of the entire family is served by giving priority to the neediest members. But our political thought is governed by liberal individualism so that society, unlike the family, is thought to be composed of masses of individuals who are essentially equal, who exist in competition with each other for available resources, and whose actions are governed by self-interest.[8] Within such a framework, the preferential option for the poor or needy can only be understood as disruptive of both order and justice. A preference for any one group or individual serves to disadvantage all others with whom that individual or group is in competition, and is therefore understood as unfair. Furthermore, this competitive advantage removes the necessity, and therefore frequently the incentive, for the preferred individual or group to compete. It then becomes very possible that a preferential option for those who are poor or needy actually disadvantages them in the long run by diminishing their incentive to compete and achieve, and making them dependent for survival upon that preference.

Rarely do those who understand political society in this way ever confront the conflict concerning human nature that exists between their conceptions of familial and political relations.[9] If preference for the poor and needy within political society disadvantages the needy by removing their incentive to achieve, surely such preference within the family would also disadvantage those needy members. Why should we try to diminish the inequities among siblings if the very weakness of some is their incentive to achieve equally against others? And yet it is impossible to convince parents who love their children that they should not expend extra efforts on their neediest children. Conflict within popular understandings of human nature in the private and the public realms emerges not only in attitudes toward preferential option, but in many other areas as well. Many persons understand democracy as normative in the public realm, yet unnecessary and counterproductive in the private realm such as the family or church.[10] Others understand moral criteria to be essential for the private realm, but impossibly utopian for government and business. We have no common understanding of human nature, no common anthropology, to draw on in our social discourse. Significant disagreements over preferential option for the poor, therefore, should not surprise us.

MISUNDERSTANDINGS OF PREFERENTIAL OPTION

There is probably no other Christian teaching which is so radically misunderstood as the preferential option. In addition to confusions about the form God's justice takes in the world, and about who God's preferential option might include, three of the most common political misunderstandings of preferential option are: (1) that it involves special privileges for the poor, (2) that it claims the poor have greater merit than the non-poor, and (3) that it is a rigorous demand made only on the non-poor.

Contrary to popular opinion, preferential option for the poor does not entail substituting privileges to compensate for the neediness of the poor, but rather entails redressing their very deprivation. Preferential option for the poor does not rest on any special claims of merit for the poor; it is neither earned nor deserved. Nor is preferential option for the poor an obligation primarily for the non-poor; in fact, preferential option demands much more from the poor themselves than from the non-poor.

Not the Substitution of Privileges

It is important to be very concrete when we talk about preferential option for the poor. Within the family, a preferential option for the poor would support using a disproportionate share of the family's health budget to obtain surgical correction of birth defects, or the treatment and cure of debilitating disease, for an affected child. It would entail extra efforts in teaching the brain-damaged child to read, to learn to be as self-sufficient as possible. It would *not* entail, for example, treating a child differently in all areas of family life in order to compensate to the child for his or her disability. To give this child more affection, more outings, exemption from normal family rules about meals, bedtimes, and behavior is not preferential option for the poor, but is rather to disadvantage this child out of misplaced pity and guilt. It is to teach that the child is essentially different from the others, and that what is special about this child is her or his lameness. It is to encourage the child to use lameness to fulfill needs, rather than to encourage the child to be normal and to overcome, so far as possible, the disability. Real preferential option for the poor is about removing the poverty of the affected individuals with the goal of making them whole and restoring them to equality and participation in the human community.

In the same way in political society, preferential option is not about giving privileges to the poor, but about removing their poverty. In our society many of the mistaken understandings of preferential option stem from an identification of preferential option with liberal support of the welfare system. The welfare system as it exists in our society is not a manifestation of preferential option. The welfare system functions not so much in the interests of eliminating poverty, as in the interest of maintaining the poor in a dependency which effectively discourages them from protesting and demanding redress of the economic system which has excluded them.[11] It is society's way of buying off the poor, at the same time that society denies the independence, dignity, and worth of the poor. From the very beginning of the welfare system, each development/extension was created to deal with a general economic crisis in which it was recognized that there was not sufficient work to go around. Welfare offered a way to prevent the mass of unemployed people from fomenting structural changes in the economy.[12] And yet the very society that created a system to substitute for the lack of work is suspicious of those on welfare, and in many ways despises them as less than human.

The mass of the poor in this society have been excluded from human work. This is the source of their poverty, in all the senses of that word. The welfare system offers an income in place of work. But income, though necessary for physical survival, is not sufficient to develop or maintain humanity. Work serves two other important functions for human beings: self-creation and social contribution/participation.[13] Work is the principal activity through which we create ourselves as persons. It is through work that we develop our talents and discover new ones; it is in work that we learn social-interaction skills. It is in work that we come to recognize who we have become and are becoming. In addition to its creative aspect, work is also the chief mechanism through which we contribute to and participate in the wider society. Our ability to take pride in who we are, to appreciate our own self-worth, is grounded in the work that we do and its role in maintaining our larger community.

Welfare or any income system which replaces work with income alone is, over the long run, destructive of individuals and communities. Welfare systems are necessary in order to prevent economic suffering when there is temporary economic dislocation, when a worker becomes sick or disabled, or too elderly to work, but it is not an effective substitute for providing work to the able.

Popular attitudes toward welfare recognize the destructiveness of substituting income for work, but misinterpret the source of the destructiveness. Permanent welfare is destructive of humanity not because it takes away the economic incentive to work and allows persons to indulge natural urges toward idleness and dependency. The need to work is not something external to human beings; work is not something our basic natures have to be forced into doing. Work is rather a need of the human soul as well as of the body. Permanent welfare destroys by omission, in that it offers persons no way to create, express and therefore discover who they are, no way to contribute to the wider human community and to feel connected to that society by one's contribution. It destroys the ability to take pride in who one is, the ability to feel integrally connected to others, the ability to experience one's life as meaningful.

The absence of work is not a privilege, but a deprivation. This is much clearer to some than to others, but even many who understand this truth in their own lives fail to see it with reference to the poor. The workaholic phenomenon is very common in our culture: the person, usually male, totally defines himself through his work and is totally absorbed in that work. There are tremendous numbers of individuals who persist in workaholic lifestyles despite public recognition of greatly enhanced possibilities of early death from heart attacks and strokes, of estranged marriages and broken homes, and of high levels of depression and alienation stemming from a lack of personal intimacy. Many insist that even, and perhaps especially, the most prestigious work in our society is designed in such a way as to exclude all but those willing to become workaholics. Many corporate law firms, for example, expect young attorneys to work seven days a week, ten hours a day. Many business executives face these same expectations. Residency programs for doctors often incorporate long work weeks combined with long periods of on-duty time in which sleep is irregular if possible at all. By the time these high pressure years are past, the pattern is set for many of these professionals, and is extremely difficult to break, even when the worker recognizes and resents such patterns.

Most of us define ourselves through our work. The first question we ask when we meet a person is usually "What do you do?" We describe ourselves as teachers, lawyers, bank tellers, plumbers, secretaries, and telephone installers. How could we fail to understand the importance of work in human life? We know that statistics show that job loss and retirement often bring on illness and even death, especially for men, who feel lost and useless without their work and the meaning and structure it provides for their lives.[14]

But many of us also feel a great resentment of work. What is not clear is that at its base it is not resentment of work itself, but resentment of the form that work takes in our society. Resentment against work is directly related to the type of work done. Polls and studies have long shown that the most desirable jobs are not always the most highly paid, but those which provide greater opportunities for independence, for service, for interaction, and for self-development, in addition to adequate compensation. Jobs such as teaching, for example, though often not paid as well as many unionized blue-collar jobs, for years ranked far above them in terms of popular desirability precisely because they were perceived, whatever the reality, as allowing for individuality and growth.[15] This has only changed in recent decades as the salary level for teachers has failed to keep pace with minimal middle-class living standards. Those jobs which are least desirable are not only those that are worst paid, but those that are the most repetitive, the most restrictive of human interaction and creativity. Within many assembly plants, high rates of absenteeism and turnover are the rule and have been for decades.[16]

Alienation from work permeates much of our society; it is not merely the result of factory organization, though it is perhaps best recognized there. Much white-collar clerical work is also characterized by repetition, by the absence of possibilities for advancement, by models of supervision that treat workers as children, making decisions for them as to when they can eat, talk, go to the bathroom, or how they can dress. Many workplaces go to great lengths to emphasize the distinctions between types of work, and the relative lack of status of some work, and therefore some workers. An example is the law firm which every year has family day at a huge amusement park, but always chooses one day for the attorneys and their families, and another day for the secretaries and clerks. There are two work days lost instead of one, for when the attorneys picnic, the secretaries and clerks have little, if anything to do at the office, and when the secretaries and clerks picnic, the attorneys can get no work out. Many firms and institutions choose similar petty ways to reinforce the relative worthlessness of low status work, as exemplified by separate rest rooms for executives and staff, or faculty and secretaries, or supervisors and rank and file employees.

To the extent that our society structures some work in ways that prevent workers from fulfilling the purposes of human work, we create attitudes of hatred toward work, and force people to accept these jobs only out of economic necessity. It is not difficult to understand how persons in such work resent welfare systems for the poor that provide income without work. But these workers, too, are among the needy, the poor, those who are deprived of full humanity because they are deprived of power to control their lives. Preferential option for the poor is a commitment to improve their lot as well.

Preferential option for the poor cannot mean the expansion of welfare systems if welfare continues to be a replacement for opportunities to work. Welfare systems maintain poverty of spirit in its most destructive forms. Preferential option is a commitment to the elimination of poverty, to the freeing of the poor to be fully human, not a commitment to merely alleviate some of the physical consequences of poverty while leaving untouched the essence of poverty—its inability to nurture true human personhood.

The Poor Are Not More Deserving

We often understand preferential option as entailing privileges for the poor because we understand it to mean that theologically, God prefers the poor because of their greater merit, their greater virtue. This seems to many who observe the poor, to be incomprehensible, for they see that among the poor there is violence, despair, irresponsibility, alcoholism, drug abuse, crime, and other forms of brokenness.

But God's preferential option for the poor is not based on any special merit on the part of the poor. Our God has always made clear, since God first elected the Hebrew slaves of Egypt as chosen people, that divine favor was bestowed not because persons deserved it, but because they needed it to redress their suffering. God's favor is bestowed on the basis of need and need alone. And God's favor is active. God did not say to the Hebrew people: "I take pity on you because of your suffering; from now on I will feel the lash with you, and distract you from your distress at the empty bellies of your children." Instead, God acted to release them from the condition which caused their suffering.

Preferential option for the poor engenders resentment in many because we want very much to believe in temporal retribution, that rewards and punishments for our actions are given in this life. We want to believe that the poor are responsible for their poverty, that we are all equally able to provide for ourselves, and that the failure to do so is a personal fault. We want to believe this for a variety of reasons. If we are not ourselves needy, belief in temporal retribution persuades us that we are therefore virtuous, that our welfare is the proof of our virtue.

In the economic arena, many who have, through great sacrifice and effort, achieved a measure of economic security and comfort want to believe that they have earned their comfort and security. In one sense this is, of course, true. But it is not true that effort and sacrifice always produce comfort and security, or that those who have not achieved such comfort and security have failed to invest effort and sacrifice. Two farmers may work just as hard, make just as many sacrifices. But one may have to contend with destructive forces beyond human control, such as a drought, a raise in interest rates, a fall in crop prices in the year of greatest vulnerability, and the other may have more luck. Two students may work just as hard in their college careers, but one may also have to contend with full-time work in order to pay tuition and living expenses, or support his invalid parents, or support children of her own. These outside pressures can mean the difference between success or failure in one's efforts.

Not only do people interpret their successes as solely the result of their virtue, but they assume that since their success proves their virtue, they do not need to fear misfortune in the future. Because we blind ourselves to the random misfortunes which afflict others, we feel safe from being victims of random misfortune ourselves. A classic example is response to rape. We tend to respond to accounts of rape by searching for ways to blame the rape victim: where was she, why was she alone, what did she do to encourage him? For if we can find some way in which she may be responsible for the rape, then other women, those who do not encourage men, those who do not go out alone, or accept rides/dates with strangers, are safe. Women who have never been raped can feel safe rather than vulnerable if the victims are responsible for their rapes.[17]

We insist on temporal retribution not only because it makes us, who are comfortable, feel virtuous and safe from misfortune, but also because it allows us to deny responsibility for redressing the misfortunes of others. If the poor are responsible for their own situation, then there is no obligation on our part to render them any assistance. To render assistance is not only not obligatory, but is actually to obstruct God's will within a scheme of temporal retribution. For if God so created the world that people are punished for lack of effort, to remove God's intended punishment for their offense would be to deny the authority of God.

The gratuitousness of God's love is very difficult for most of us to accept. In our experience, persons are generally accepted, included, or rewarded on the basis of what they have to offer, not gratuitously. We come to expect that we will be treated on the basis of our power, wealth, achievements, and general merit. But each of us has a need to be loved and accepted solely for who we are, to have our needs met because we are important regardless of what we have done or what we have to offer. The rich man may flaunt his wealth, the beautiful woman her looks, in order to attract other people, but both of them have a need to be loved without reference to wealth or appearance, to be loved in ways which will survive the loss of wealth or beauty. We insist on established patterns of relating based on merit and achievement not because these are ultimately satisfying, but because we have been well socialized in them. We may be afraid to believe that gratuitous love or regard are possible, lest we be disappointed. We may have suffered so much from past evaluations of our lack of merit that when we have achieved the merit based on which we can demand the regard of others, we may think of their regard as our due. Conversion to a recognition and acceptance of the gratuitous love of God includes a face-to-face encounter with our inmost self which yearns for gratuity.

Preferential option makes no claims for either exclusive or permanent preference for the poor. Critics of liberation theology often reject preferential option for the poor because they assume that it is based on merit. This is why very often their criticism focuses on refuting the statements made by liberation theologians about the faith of the poor. Critics insist that the faith of the poor will weaken when their condition improves, demonstrating that they are no more worthy of God's preferential option than the non-poor.[18] This criticism entirely misses the point. The poor have God's special option solely on the basis of need—neither these individuals nor the condition of poverty are meritorious in themselves. God loves all equally, and so should we. Among those loved, the preference in deciding and acting must go to those who are in need at the moment. When a group of the poor have been successful over time in redressing the wounds with which poverty afflicted them, they cease to be poor, and lose the place of priority to those who are still poor. For most of us, then, preferential option does not exclude us in favor of other people, so much as it requires that we share the place of privilege with others depending upon whose needs are greater at the time. Some will remain more or less constantly in the preferred group—but who among the non-poor would opt to trade places with those who by virtue of their constant powerlessness and suffering receive God's preferred concern?

Though there is a connection between the preferential option for the poor and the hermeneutic (or epistemological) privilege claimed by liberation theologians for the poor (the poor's greatest openness to and knowledge of God), the former is not based on the latter. Preferential option is based on the neediness of the poor. The hermeneutic or epistemological privilege is the result of two factors. One is the fact that poverty itself deprives the poor of many of the idols (alternative sources of security and meaning) which tempt the non-poor from faithful recognition of their dependence on God's gratuitous love.[19] But the second factor which produces the epistemological privilege of the poor is struggle against poverty. For poverty itself, as an evil, kills bodies and souls, distorts and thwarts the human personality, all of which constitute obstacles to knowledge and experience of God. It is in commitment to the struggle against poverty that the poor become linked to God in common cause, and therefore know God better. For this reason, epistemological privilege is not the common property of the poor, but a characteristic specific to those poor who struggle against poverty, as Hugo Assmann reminds us.[20]

Greater Demands Are Made On The Non-Poor

While working within Christian churches and religious-education programs over the last decade, I gradually came to see that there is tremendous popular ambivalence about preferential option for the poor rooted in commonly shared notions of justice. For some years I interpreted this as the ignored child accusing the parent or teacher of favoritism toward another, as exemplifying the resentment of the elder son in the parable of the prodigal son. This element is certainly present in many responses to preferential option for the poor. But in the last few years I have come to see that a great deal of popular Christian ambivalence about preferential option for the poor stems from a sound conviction that all persons are called to conversion and discipleship, including the poor. When we say, as we increasingly do in the Christian churches, that preferential option for the poor provides both the starting point and the structure for the process of conversion and discipleship, we leave many persons with the impression that the poor are excluded from this process. For the non-poor in the churches understand preferential option for the poor as only binding on the non-poor. Preferential option obliges them to commit themselves to the welfare of the poor. But how does a commitment to the poor challenge the poor to conversion? to discipleship? If preferential option for the poor is the core of conversion and discipleship, then these have diminished meaning for the poor, who can proceed with life as usual. But life as usual is not Christian life. So how can preferential option be the core of conversion and discipleship?

The mistake is in thinking that the preferential option is addressed only to the non-poor—it is addressed to all, and it is both meaningful and challenging to all. In fact, it is much more difficult for the poor than for the non-poor. The failure to understand the challenge to the poor in preferential option for the poor is the result of abysmal ignorance of the poor on the part of the non-poor.

Life as usual for the poor is no more centered on the elimination of poverty than is life as usual among the non-poor. Life as usual among the poor can be a struggle to survive from day to day, a struggle to escape from the condition of poverty through hard work or crime, or a surrender to temporary escapes from the ravages of poverty through alcohol, drugs, or mental illness. Preferential option for the poor, on the other hand, challenges the poor to leave behind the temporary mental escapes, to forgo schemes designed to engineer individual paths from poverty, and to take on the struggle against poverty itself—to free all the poor from poverty.

The powerlessness which afflicts the varied groups of the poor is the result of their exclusion from social decision making. They are not a part of the negotiation between social groups which determines social policy. Even when social decision making claims to take into account the needs of the poor—women, racial minorities, the unemployed, the handicapped, the mentally ill—these groups are not consulted, and their perspective is not included. Thousands of people who are mentally ill roam the streets of our cities because legal decisions, supposedly made to insure that their rights were not ignored, mandated their release in the absence of specific treatment plans. There was not, and still is not, an adequate attempt to meet the special needs of mentally ill people in our health-care system. Provisions for group homes and halfway houses, employment, job training—none of these are adquate for the numbers of people released from mental institutions to the danger of the streets, where they are prey to thieves, drug addicts, hunger, and cold.

Welfare and unemployment programs have an abysmal record of consulting the needs and experiences of the needy during their planning. There is a general assumption that such people are not competent to define what they need. Job training programs for women, especially programs for training women for executive positions, have rarely consulted women, or those who research the skills and perspective of women returning to work, in constructing these programs. The assumption is that men who are successful executives are the experts, and that women should follow the male model. Women should be like men, those who are handicapped like those who are normal, the mentally ill like the healthy, the unemployed like the employed. The non-poor draw up the plans for the poor, and when the plans do not work, the fault is that of the poor, for they are obviously either not capable, or not willing to invest the necessary effort.

The demand of the preferential option for the poor that those who are poor commit themselves to the elimination of poverty of all types clearly demands that they work to insert themselves into the decision-making processes of society, that they change social institutions so that these institutions work for the poor as they do for the non-poor. At a very material level, such a task requires *organization, leadership*, the development of extensive *social analysis*, and the ability to make coalitions with other groups, none of which come easily to the poor. At a *psychic* level, the preferential option for the poor requires that the poor develop confidence in their abilities, acquire self-respect and respect for others like themselves, and learn to overcome their fear of anger.

1. Organization.   The poor of all types are inherently unorganized. This is one of the reasons for their powerlessness. In North America the poor are isolated individuals and enclaves in the midst of the majority non-poor. How does one go about organizing the handicapped, much less the unemployed? The very experience of being handicapped, or unemployed, is one of being different, of being the one who stands out from all others. Others are alike, and I am different, and less in some way.

Hispanics, blacks, and other racial or ethnic minorities are exceptions to this usual rule, but even for them organization is a dismaying task. Blacks discovered in the experience of the civil rights movement that blacks have almost no social institutions of their own. The black church became the rallying point of the civil rights movement largely by default, because it, more than any other institution found in the black community, was controlled by blacks, had a trained leadership core, and represented large parts of the community.[21] Even so, the task of organization was overwhelming, and the civil rights movement proved to be more effective at striking down obstacles blocking blacks from access to such formal rights as voting, than at organizing blacks to form coalitions which could use their voting power to change other institutions.

Hispanics, most of whom are Catholic, do not have an institution similar to the black church. The majority of Catholic priests in Hispanic parishes are not Hispanic; there are very few Hispanic bishops in the United States; and the Catholic church, unlike independent black churches, is extremely hierarchical with power located in the bishops and Vatican, rather than in the congregational level.

Nonracial groups of the powerless tend to be even less cohesive. Even the economically poor are extremely difficult to organize. Some groups among them are impossible to organize on any long-term basis—the homeless, for example, are itinerant. But the homeless are not alone in their mobility.[22] The economically poor not only tend to move from address to address, depending on whether they can afford rent or must live with relatives or friends, or where the latest job is. Their poverty also tends to be erratic. For example, over half the welfare recipients in the nation average less than two consecutive years on welfare. Most move back-and-forth between short term jobs and welfare.[23]

Besides mobility problems, the poor tend to have no experience with organizing. Most of their experience with organizations has been alienating. They do not understand common social institutions as benign, but as foreign, and in many cases hostile.

Police, social workers, hospitals, schools, and other social institutions with which the poor are familiar are viewed with ambivalence if not suspicion. These same institutions can often be experienced as disapproving and hostile to the desire of the poor to empower themselves and exercise social power with other groups. People who are handicapped often characterize schools, hospitals, and social agencies as contributing to their handicap by teaching dependency and acceptance, by exercising power over them in paternalistic ways rather than enabling them to learn independence. Those mired in generations of poverty often experience social workers as persons hired to supervise the maintenance of their poverty, the police as hostile, suspicious and harassing, and the schools as dumping grounds for kids going nowhere.

Most non-poor understand social institutions as benign; police, social agencies, schools, hospitals, and the media are all assumed to answer their social needs. Many of the powerless understand political parties as manipulative, promising to meet the needs of the poor in order to obtain their support, and abandoning them when in power. The media virtually never depicts reality from the perspective of the powerless; the powerful present much more attractive, articulate, and persuasive spokespersons for their views than do the poor. All these social institutions can and are turned against powerless people who step out of their assigned roles and dare to try to change their society.

2. *Lack of Leadership.*   In addition to a lack of experience with organizing, and suspicions of organized groups, the poor do not have a leadership core. There are, of course, capable individuals among the poor who have natural talents in leadership. But few have leadership experience, and virtually none in sustained organizations of the poor themselves.[24]

For most of the poor, leaders seem to be people unlike themselves. Leaders are powerful, effective, self-confident. The self-doubt that our social system produces in the poor makes the poor distrust other poor as leaders. For if the social system teaches the handicapped that they are not whole, that they are dependent, if it teaches women that they are not truly rational, but only emotional, if it teaches the unemployed that if they were worthy, they would have jobs, then the social system teaches these people a form of self-hate. This message is very effective. Women are less likely than men to support women for the most responsible leadership positions. Unemployed people are often more suspicious than others of persons in the same circumstances. If we have internalized messages about our own unworthiness, or about our own responsibility for our neediness, then we are unlikely to respect those who share our characteristics. But if the poor cannot respect other poor, if the poor cannot expect real leadership from them, if they insist that leaders come from outside, then the poor undermine their very cause. For the outsider cannot really know the perspective of those in the situation.

Furthermore, unless the poor can reject the dominant social messages of our society, their understanding of leadership is likely to be at odds with attempts to eliminate poverty. For the dominant message about leadership is that it is a form of domination, of coercion, of controlling people. The leader is the one with power over others. Groups which have little experience with organization often uncritically mirror the forms of authority in the society which marginalizes them. They turn on the leaders they have created in this image when it becomes clear that such leaders do not empower their followers, but only imitate the dominant society in manipulating the poor.

The real situation is that the poor have the least training for leadership and the worst social models of leaders—as controllers. Yet these poor are called by preferential option for the poor to develop leaders who will use their power to empower others, who will neither be co-opted by the material rewards nor by the status offered by the dominant groups, and who will refrain from all forms of coercion and manipulation.

3. *Social Analysis.* Commitment to preferential option for the poor entails choosing both goals and strategies. Goals should be based on needs; strategies demand social analysis. Some goals should be sought before others because they are possible sooner, because it is important to demonstrate to the poor that they can be effective, and because some victories can pave the way for related victories in the future. Before choosing strategies the poor must analyze their society. If the plan is to eliminate homelessness, for example, it is necessary to investigate: What is the history of this problem? Has it always existed? Where did the various groups of the homeless come from? What factors lead persons out of homelessness, and which groups are most affected? Is there a shortage of housing? Of low cost housing? If so, why? What causes such shortages? Who benefits from homelessness, if anyone? What forces maintain homelessness? When we examine the history of homelessness, what trends are visible? What can we expect in the future?

Social analysis is intimidating. Social reality is complex, and no issue exists in isolation. There is great expertise available for social analysis, but this has the effect of confusing many persons and making them think that social analysis is a job for experts. "The paralysis of analysis," Martin Luther King Jr., called this phenomenon. But we do social analysis all the time. We analyze reality before and after we make decisions. We usually analyze small pieces of reality, those closest to us, but we do analysis. We do it when we search for a job, when we try to understand election results, when we decide where we want to live, when we try and decide what trends are going to affect our future, and what shape they take at the moment.

The poor do not have great access to the formal tools of social analysis. Few understand complex statistical data on ownership contraction (contraction in the size of the pool of land owners—an increasing contraction of ownership into the hands of a few) or on patterns of economic development. But the trends that such data supports are not news to the poor. Most women are convinced by their experience that our society is still misogynist. The handicapped early suspect that debate about their right to access various institutions depends on how much that right will cost business, cities, and public agencies. Racial minorities have very astute opinions as to why unemployment becomes a nonissue in politics when the rate goes down to the point where most affected are minorities. But there is resistence on the part of many of the poor to doing thorough social analysis. The poor often distrust experts, especially intellectuals. The language of experts seems designed to confuse and obfuscate, and the powerless suspect that such confusion and obfuscation empower the experts at the expense of the powerless.

The poor are often right in this suspicion. But the need of the poor for social analysis in preferential option for the poor does not mean that the poor need to hire a social analyst and accept his or her analysis. Instead, the real task is to try to broaden the already existing image they have of society, attempting to include the perspective of all the poor, to make it internally consistent, to test it against whatever data they can put together, and to continue to refine it through group reflection on experience as they proceed with strategy. Social analysis is for all the poor to do, and to redo and redo. When social analysis is done by groups as a whole, the potential leadership core is enlarged, the mass of the poor can more responsibly take part in decisions, lessening their dependence on the leadership—and the poor become less poor because they become less powerless. But this is a tremendous task.

4. Psychic Resources. Preferential option for the poor is demanding, and sometimes dangerous for the poor at two levels. Preferential option threatens to increase their powerlessness at both a material and a psychic level. For preferential option for the poor calls the poor—the unemployed, the underemployed, disadvantaged racial minorities, the sick and handicapped, battered women, abused children, and all other relatively powerless groups—to collective action on behalf of all those similarly affected. Many of these people already live at the edge, in a day-to-day struggle to put food on the table, to avoid those who do them violence, to find the strength to go on to the next day. While some live in hope of a future that is better, many live with real fear for the future, unable to believe that the future holds more than the suffering and degradation of the past. Preferential option for the poor demands that they transfer their energies and activities from individual strategies for survival to collective strategies of social transformation.

It is much harder for the poor to transfer their allegiance to collective struggle than it is for the non-poor. The non-poor in the United States take for granted that social institutions work largely in their interests, that they are the majority, and that others will continue to represent their interests within the institutions of society. Even if the non-poor do accept some risk to their own welfare through commitment to the struggle against poverty, they have a much greater margin of safety between them and serious risk than do the poor.

The poor are much more likely to feel at risk from commitment to the struggle against poverty. When poor blacks and Hispanics organize into groups to demand enforcement of housing laws in urban ghettos, they know that the landlords they oppose are powerful. They know that such action is likely to lead to dangerous unexplained fires in the middle of the night, to anonymous calls reporting immigration violations among the tenants, to pressure on local employers to fire tenants involved in the action, as well as, of course, evictions. When the underemployed attempt to organize to force an employer to pay proportionate benefits, or to pay them on the books so that the employer pays Social Security taxes for them, they know that the result is likely to be that reasons are invented for firing the primary organizers. Members of the non-poor who involve themselves in such campaigns invest their time, energy, and sometimes money, but the risk is not, and cannot be, shared equally. For the poor it is often much safer to resign oneself to being victimized, or to invest oneself in individual efforts to escape the situation, for example, through another job, or another apartment. Is it any wonder that movements of the poor, no matter how great the needs of the poor, fail to attract all the poor? For many, even a life of deprivation appears less demanding and less risky.

Even when the poor and the non-poor join together in an effort to eliminate some form of powerlessness, the poor are more vulnerable to reprisals. They are both more visible and more defenseless against institutions opposing structural changes. In the civil rights movement poor blacks were dependent for bail money on the underfunded movement itself, while white protesters and affluent blacks could bail out of the jails.

Furthermore, the poor are aware of their greater vulnerability. It often happens that the non-poor can be drawn into the first stages of a preferential option for the poor without fully realizing the path on which they tread. They volunteer a few hours a week at a food pantry, or a shelter for the homeless. Sometimes their compassion for victims and their anger at injustice have drawn them deeply into the struggle for change before they realize what radical changes this commitment entails in their worldview and lifestyle. Such gradual dawning of the risk is much rarer among the poor, who are much more aware that their situation is not so much an oversight or an exception within the overall society, but rather the result of a structural blindness necessary to protect the overall system. The poor have learned to expect backlash when the system is challenged. They see the world as divided into two sides. It is only the non-poor who have afforded the luxury of imagining their lot as systemically independent of that of the poor. The poor therefore have more reason to hesitate in the face of preferential option because they understand better the immense task confronting preferential option and the extensive risk involved in that task. Those who have been given the least experience of achieving goals, of garnering recognition of their worth and talents—the least experience of success—have fewer material resources and psychic reserves with which to approach such a task. And yet throughout history steps toward justice for the poor—for the marginated, the powerless, the despised—have rarely come about without precipitating action from the poor undertaken with great sacrifice and risk. Preferential option for the poor is more demanding of the poor than of the non-poor, but their greater need for the relief of the kingdom of God, toward which preferential option moves human society, can, under the right historical circumstances, compensate for the greater risks entailed and motivate groups of the poor to commit themselves to preferential option.

But where in our churches do we hear any of this? Too often the message that all of us, poor and non-poor alike, are brothers and sisters, children of the same God is the sole theological basis for the Christian obligation for preferential option for the poor. But our common status as children of God is not sufficient to make the non-poor able to engage in *effective* preferential option. Too often the non-poor who are motivated by such a message to engage in preferential option are soon disgusted with the hesitancy of the poor, their self-doubt, their difficulty with solidarity and effective leadership, and their battle with despair. A middle-class friend of mine engaged in a training program for women assisting rape victims reported midway through the training that she had tremendous difficulty dealing with the attitudes of many rape victims. She found it impossible to understand or identify with their self-blame, their lack of anger, their fear of reporting, of the police and court system, their acceptance—in spite of their fear and suffering—of their violation as part of the way the world works. She reported that almost a third of her training class had dropped out due to their inability to identify with such victims. She said, "I went into this program to help my sisters, but I have a lot of trouble feeling like a sister to women who respond like this."

It is not enough for the churches to teach that we are sisters and brothers to the poor. We need to learn about sin—that sin is not merely disobeying a divine command, it is not merely offending God, as if God's desires for human beings are entirely arbitrary. Sin offends God because it harms persons, it distorts the humanity of those it victimizes, it wounds those whom God loves. Addressing sin entails more than obtaining contrition from the sinner, more than the cessation of the sinful action. Sin is not erased when God forgives the sinner. Sins of theft are not the only sins which require restitution. Restitution is about making whole the victims of sin, and this restitution requires more than returning whatever money or material possessions are stolen. How does one make whole the lives of entire communities of the poor in which over half the adults are unemployed, ten percent of the men are addicts, one in twenty babies are born HIV positive, one in twenty persons are homeless, and two thirds of the adolescents do not finish high school? Restitution involves more than supplying that which was originally refused. Even if one could introduce adequately paid full-time jobs, bring the housing up to code, and provide adequate medical care for those dying in the corridors of understaffed hospitals, the damage done lives on in addiction and anger, despair and hostility, self-blame and distrust. Restitution to the victims of poverty is a complex process often extending to generations.

Preferential option for the poor cannot be effectively taught—which means that the gospel cannot be effectively taught—unless we teach the consequences of sin for victims as an integral part of the meaning of sin. For too long the churches have taught the consequences of sin to the sinner only, and emphasized that damnation can always be avoided by repentance since God's love is gratuitous and merciful, bestowed upon all willing to accept it. We have debates in the churches about whether sinners are better motivated to avoid and repent of sin by church emphasis on the punishment waiting for sinners, or by church emphasis on God's ready forgiveness for sin. But if we really want to understand God's forgiveness we have to ask how God would have responded to the priest and the Levite who passed by the man beaten and robbed by thieves, if the Samaritan had not come along, if the man died, if his wife and children were sold into slavery for failure to produce the stolen money to pay off debt, if in slavery they were separated, beaten and starved, and succumbed to suicide or brutality? What does God's preferential option for the poor imply about forgiveness of the priest and the Levite? God is not ignorant of the mechanics of sin and its affects on human beings. Neither can we afford to be.

CHAPTER 3

ENDING THE
ROMANTICIZATION
OF VICTIMS

According to the theory of Italian marxist Antonio Gramsci, ruling elites remain in place so long as their ideology can convince the masses that existing structures work in their interests better than any present alternative.[1] Many leftists, following Gramsci, hold that rule by force has a limited effectiveness; any political system to be stable must convince the masses, or at least the greater part of the masses, of its legitimacy. Since ruling elites have as their first priority the protection of their own disproportionate political and economic status which is incompatible with the interests of the masses, ruling elites, and elites which aspire to rule, use emotional appeals to traditional values, fears, and aspirations of the masses to establish legitimacy. Some common appeals used by ruling elites recently are to concepts such as patriotism, social order, motherhood and family, anticommunism, sexual complementarity, sacrificial heroism, and traditional religion/morality.

Leftists, those who propose various egalitarian alternatives to ruling elites, must then, in order to displace ruling elites, combat false consciousness by debunking the ruling ideology and unveiling the systemic material exploitation of the masses by the elites. Gramsci maintained that the left had not only the critical task of debunking ideology and exposing systemic exploitation, but also a constructive task of presenting the masses with a workable alternative system compatible with the vision underlying the critique of the present system.

In our world today we are accustomed to seeing the left of center political spectrum debunking the right's use of motherhood, the flag and apple pie to defend an unequal system. The left often understands romanticism—the idealization and use of certain aspects of reality as symbols—as characteristic of the right, whether we refer to Reagan, the new religious right, the Cold War rhetoric of the fifties and sixties, the right-to-life movement, or to the law and order movement of the late sixties and seventies.

But romanticism is not always a tool of the right. It is not only the Reagans and Pinochets, the Falwells and Robertsons, the Hitlers and Mussolinis, the Schafflys and Bryants who use romanticism to appeal to the emotions of the masses. Nor is romanticism limited to the right and to populists such as William Jennings Bryan or Juan Peron. The left has used romanticism, too. And the use of romanticism is dangerous, even deadly, for the left.

One reason that romanticism is such a temptation to the left is that the masses they must address are already characterized by a false consciousness attuned to emotional appeals. The alternative to the use of romanticism is political education. Political education entails a long process in which people learn to discern their true material interests and to unmask the ways in which they are manipulated by idealized symbols which appeal to their fears and values. Because romanticism has been so effective with the masses, and because it has left them attuned to emotional appeals, it can easily appear to those who desire change as a short cut to political power through bypassing the lengthy political education phase.

The left's use of romanticism is deadly, first because the use of romanticism can only undermine moves toward egalitarianism. For as a tool of manipulation, romanticism is inherently elitist. Second, given romanticism's failure to politically educate the masses to their own true interests, the loyalty of the masses can only be temporary and partial. It can be lost as soon as the right dreams up some new appeal to people's deepest fears and aspirations. And the left is necessarily more handicapped than the right in fighting political wars using romanticism. To be true to itself the left must be loyal to everyone; the right is loyal only to the ruling elite. It therefore has greater freedom to play groups off against one another, to use the fears, prejudices, and intolerances of one group against others. The right can win by appealing to fear; the left must win by appealing to hope and solidarity, both of which must be built.

Political education using social analysis is, in the long run, a much more potent tool for the left. The left must use history and social science to demonstrate the process of exploitation and control in a way that explains to the masses their own experiences and dissatisfactions.

Once the romantic mask is removed, the right is basically reduced to
two arguments: that what is has been ordained, and that attempts to
restructure reality can produce only chaos.

Social analysis demands reasoning. Yet it is simplistic to assume
that the left must use reason, the right emotion, in pitching successful
appeals to mass audiences. No good social analysis fails to engage the
emotions. In fact, the first reaction of many—from the base level to
social analysis unmasking their manipulation—is anger.[2] This is an
appropriate reaction. We *should* feel anger at injustice, at exploitation. The anger both represents and generates energy, the energy to
make things right. An egalitarian order must not only appeal to our
reason regarding our material interests, but must also satisfy basic
emotional needs—needs for dignity, security, solidarity, equality,
and creativity.

Because of the dualistic division of reason and emotion in western
culture, we have tended to speak of emotion disparagingly, and to
elevate reason. Marxism's attempt, especially after Engels,[3] to present Marxism as a science, and to concentrate on the material (economic) level was a reaction against the romanticism and idealization
characterizing political ideology of the nineteenth century, but it
unfortunately was overinfluenced by this separation of reason and
emotion, resulting in the frequent failure to be explicit about non-
material needs. Today criticism of romanticism is often interpreted as
an attack on emotion and an endorsement of reason alone. But romanticism and emotion are not synonymous. Romanticism is distorted use
of emotion. It originates in the unnatural separation of emotion from
reason, a separation which deforms emotion by uprooting it from reality so that it is easily captured and manipulated for political purposes
by any group for whom it seems convenient.

BEGINNINGS OF A RELIGIOUS LEFT

Our society has begun to see the involvement of religiously-motivated
persons and of religious communities in leftist politics. At first, it
might seem that this part of the left could be of significant help in
reuniting reason in the form of social analysis with emotion in terms
of psychic and interpersonal aspirations. Not only does religious spirituality and liturgy draw heavily on emotion, but liberal Christian
churches have been drifting for decades toward understanding church
mission in terms of meeting both personal and communal needs.

Whether religion goes left or right, it incorporates emotions. Many in the liberal churches have moved to the left, partly as a result of the integration of the theological disciples with the secular disciplines in seminaries and universities. Such training, especially when followed by job experience in various types of pastoral work involving community organizing, advocacy for the poor, and many types of popular education, has created a new religious corps of leftist activists trained in social analysis and creating political strategy. Much of the social analysis emerging from this sector is compelling.

Yet the religious left has not used the social analysis created by its intellectuals very well in its work of mass political education. On many issues the appeal of the left at the base level has instead been made in romantic terms. It is sometimes a pseudointellectual romanticism, filled with brief quotes or references to good texts or thinkers. But it is very short on reasoned approaches to reality, and long on blatant and idealized appeals to pity, and in an indirect, perverted way to violence and blood lust.

The pseudointellectual romanticism in the ranks of the Christian left to which I belong disturbs me. I see it as a tremendous threat to the liberation movements of the poor, of women and of children, and to the liberation theology arising from these groups struggling for liberation. I do not intend a criticism of liberation theology or of liberation movements of the oppressed, but a warning that popularizers can ultimately be enemies of the practitioners of liberation. The remainder of this chapter is an attempt to describe and analyze this breakdown between the level of social analytic construction and the level of political education within the religious left.

RELIGION AND ROMANTICISM

One reason that the religious left falls prey to romanticism is that western religion has often been a tool of the right. Ruling religious elites are tempted, like ruling secular elites, to use their power in order to perpetuate those structures and mechanisms which serve them and their group. Christians have too often interpreted Jesus' criticism of the misuse of religious authority in his own society as a critique of Judaism as a religion, and not as a criticism of the ability of religious elites in general to ignore the needs of the masses in favor of their own interests. The basic temptation is to identify religion with the divine—the church or Christendom with the kingdom of God on earth, the officers of the church with Christ—instead of as a means of seeking the divine. Once this identification is made, romanticism becomes a necessary tool for maintaining the identification in the minds of the masses. The divinization of the church and its officers is a first step in empowering the church to romanticize other elements of reality by linking them to the divine. Some entities can be linked to the divine in ways which empower them, as the church did for itself and for political power structures through teachings such as the divine right of kings. Other entities were defined as linked to the divine in ways which restricted their power, as has been the case for the poor. While church and political hierarchies were identified as representatives for the divine, groups such as the poor were identified as special to, chosen by, and pleasing to the divine, so that acceptance of their lot earned divine favor to be rewarded in the next life. The poor were to imitate Jesus, who was presented as accepting the difficult lot assigned to him and was rewarded with a permanent place at the right hand of God. Some Christians have, both now and in the past, resisted not only the romanticization of poverty but also the separation of humanity into two parts, one which represents God on earth and one which represents only the humanity of Jesus. But the temptation to sacralize existing relations of inequality and exploitation through such romanticization remains strong within the church.

The church's romanticization of poverty begins with interpretation of the priority of the poor for Jesus himself[4] in the Gospels. Jesus' openness to and concern for the poor and marginated in the Gospels led to more or less constant teaching within Christianity concerning the priority of concern for the poor.[5] This concern took two forms. One was an emphasis on charity or almsgiving, and eventually led to the establishment of varied institutions such as hospitals, orphanages, and poorhouses. The other was the emergence in theology of the idea that the poor were somehow closer to God than others. But both of these concerns for the poor developed in a church which understood itself as linked to the most powerful empire in the world, a linkage which conferred legitimation on the empire and protection and privilege on the church. At the same time that the Christian community of the New Testament, partly out of an attempt to escape persecution, had begun to court the powerful (which E. Schüssler Fiorenza and others demonstrate began long before the church actually took on the trappings of power from Constantine),[6] the church, caught in an otherworldly spiritual current from the East, also turned to the glorification of asceticism. Asceticism served to justify poverty as a good in itself. The poor were closer to God because they lived the ideal simple lifestyle and shared in the suffering and powerlessness of Christ, and so their reward would be greater in the kingdom to come.[7] Thus the church came to present Jesus as the poorest of the poor, born in a stable, who was also the founder of a royal church.[8] Within an imperial framework, romanticizing poverty served as the opiate which helped prevent the poor from challenging the structures of domination with which the church was allied.

Today liberation theology takes issue with past teaching. The poor are special to God because of their need. Our God cannot ignore the cries of the needy. But it is the poor *who struggle against* poverty— not those brought to despair by the sufferings of poverty—who experience closeness to God, because they are joined with God in opposition to the sinfulness of poverty. Neither the condition of poverty nor the people who suffer it are necessarily good. God's preference is not for the good, but for the needy. All human beings are called not only to share in the suffering and death of Christ, but also in the glory of the resurrection—not some of us to the suffering and some of us to the glory. Unfortunately, as we saw in chapter 2, liberation theologies are often misunderstood to be continuing the tradition of romanticizing the poor.

The churches have been very complicit in the romanticization of all three classic objects of romanticism in the West: women, children and the poor. Women and children were also objects of Jesus' special concern[9] as marginalized and powerless persons in their society, but as the church adapted to the structures of patriarchy in the following centuries they were not so idealized as the poor. Though we can point to some later instances of romanticism in the worship of Madonna and child or the courtly love tradition, the influence of gnostic body/mind dualism was so strong as to make all persons clearly defined in terms of body and nature—such as women and children—difficult to fully idealize.[10]

Full romanticization of women and children began only in reaction to the overemphasis on rationality following the Enlightenment. In the wake of industrial capitalism, new roles had to be found for women and children as they were pushed out of the world of productive labor and into new consumer roles as housekeeper and student.[11] These roles as ornaments and consumers began to develop among the upper classes centuries ago, and by the nineteenth century reached the middle class, and then the working class in the twentieth century. Modern romanticization of women and children was a result of their exclusion from the world of paid work, and an inducement, especially for women, to accept unrecognized responsibility for maintaining and reproducing the work force. Their new roles began to function as repositories for all those qualities—such as innocence, gentleness, compassion, mutuality, and vulnerability—which were not compatible with the new competitive impersonal public world but were too valuable to be lost all together.[12] Women and children were kept under control not only by the attraction of the status and privileges they received on their pedestals, but also by their perception that the contribution they provided to society, those human qualities which now reposed with them, were not only appreciated by their society, but necessary for its survival.[13] Brute force was needed even less to keep women and children in line than it had been needed against the poor; all three groups were convinced that their assigned roles were necessary, even if they did as individuals sometimes wish they could have escaped them.

ROMANTICIZING VICTIMS

In the liberation movements focused on women and children today, there are also tendencies to resort to romanticizing these groups as victims, but for lack of space here, I will limit my examples to romanticizing the poor as victims.

The classic basis for romanticizing all three has been the view of women, children, and the poor as naturally good and innocent. Closer inspection shows that what was really being idealized was their powerlessness, which for ruling elites is, of course, their virtue. Their powerlessness is, at the same time, what makes women, children, and the poor good and what makes them less than those who are unlike them, the powerful. The idealization of these groups on the grounds of their natural goodness and innocence carried with it an obligation on the part of the powerful to protect their innate goodness and innocence by preserving their powerlessness.

It has never been the case that romantic treatment of women, children, and the poor obliterated other less flattering portraits. The same writers who painted the romantic portraits were likely to describe women as devious and dishonest, children as uncivilized savages, and the poor as brutal and animal-like. But the romantic picture was understood to be what was both possible and desirable—what God desired from these groups. The romantic portrait was presented as the model, and the more negative one represented deviance from the ideal.[14]

The religious left for the most part understands how this romanticism worked. It has learned through unmasking the distinctions between doing justice and giving charity, through learning what forms of authority are compatible with servant leadership, through experiences of facilitating generation of indigenous leadership among the marginated, and through learning from the poor the intimate relationship between dignity and power. The romanticism that the religious left falls prey to is not the romanticism of the right, not the romaticization of powerless persons innately good and innocent. It is rather the idealization of victims which entraps the left. The root, again, is powerlessness, but this romanticism is motivated neither by admiration for their simplicity and malleability, nor by any conscious effort at domination. It is rather animated by a combination of revulsion at pain and suffering, pity for the victims of it, and awed admiration for their ability to endure such evil. For the left, the poor, women, and children are seen as victimized by structures which must be changed, while for the right the structures themselves are idealized, and victimization is not seen as structural and universal, but partial and accidental.

A second reason that the Christian left falls prey to romanticizing victims has less to do with the history and nature of Christianity and more to do with the phenomenon of desensitization in our culture. As a people we have become emotionally deprived, starved to feel. The alienation which characterizes our culture—alienation from others, from ourselves, from the work we do and from the natural world in which we live—has cut us off from real feeling.[15] We are especially aware of desensitization with regard to sex and violence, though these are certainly not the only subject areas. The explosion in the communications media—books, magazines, posters, billboards, radio, TV, movies—has been accompanied by an explosion in the depiction of violence and sex. In recent years, the pornography industry and parts of the advertising industry have severely escalated their depictions of violence and sexual objectification. Many psychologists, including many who deal with sex offenders, believe that constant exposure to violence, whether it be in the form of rape or war, over time desensitizes an individual's ability to feel, so that to achieve the same intensity of feeling—feelings of arousal, compassion, hatred or outrage—the degree of violence must be periodically increased.

In Margaret Atwood's *The Handmaid's Tale* a commander in the new society of the religious right in which women are sobordinates explains to his handmaid how his society is better than the society which it replaced: now that men are in total control, he says, they can feel again, which they had lost the ability to do.[16] Today this loss of the ability to feel extends beyond gender limits. People devote themselves to desperate attempts to feel real emotion. Some become thrill seekers, addicted to such things as roller coasters, ski slopes, and white-water rafting, others to soap operas that purposely overdraw all their characters, involving them in short order in every heart-wrenching predicament possible. Movies today must either thrill us with non-stop narrow escapes and car crashes, excite our bloodlust with legions of writhing bodies or bloody corpses, or make us roll with laughter at cruel satire or comedic self-parody.

If we have been desensitized to death, to sex, to laughter and peace, if we have difficulty feeling, then political education becomes more difficult. For if information is to make sense to us, to penetrate our consciousness, we must first care about it. If we are attempting to educate a church group about the effects of U.S. contra aid for Nicaragua, we must first ensure that the audience feels some small connection to the Nicaraguan people. If they don't, they won't care enough to listen to what the policy is, much less how it affects Nicaraguans. How do we most often get people to care about others? We describe the need of those others, their suffering. But over time, as people are bombarded with TV, radio, newspapers, and speakers at churches and PTAs all describing needy, suffering people, we increasingly screen out all but the most vicious suffering. Those who want us to care about their suffering victims are tempted to focus more and more on the suffering, in order to capture our attention.

The greater the suffering of victims, the more they seem to deserve our attention; the more they suffer, the more courageous, strong, and virtuous they seem. But those who suffer unjustly should not need to deserve our attention. Justice should not be distributed on the basis of merit; surely those who have received it and those who have the power to confer it did not earn it. In practical terms justice is often a precondition for achievement. In theological terms, justice exists in the realm of grace, from the gratuitousness of God's love. Merit (virtue) is a human response to the degree of justice with which we have been gifted.

Those who are desperate to feel, to be connected to others at some basic level, but who cannot face the pain in their own lives, are attracted to the extreme sufferings of others, for it allows them to feel vicariously, without the cost of firsthand pain and suffering.

In the contemporary liberation movements of all three groups, there is a general agreement on the evil of domination and exploitation, and on the value of all persons. But as we come to view the forces of domination as evil, there is a temptation to view the victims of domination as virtuous by reason of their victimization, to romanticize the victims. These groups *are* victims. But to romanticize the victims is to ignore what is essentially evil in domination, and that is its power to corrupt. Liberation can never be the work of a moment, for it requires conversion of both the victim and the oppressor. Victims have been victimized—robbed of some of their humanity—and this loss of humanity cannot be restored merely by the removal of the victims' chains.

LIBERATION THEOLOGY: NO ROMANCE

Latin American liberation theology understands this. Gustavo Gutiérrez speaks of the poor as "nonpersons," who have been deprived of opportunities to develop into fully human persons.[17] Hugo Assmann[18] insists that the epistemological privilege belongs to the communities of the poor struggling to eliminate poverty, and not to all victims of poverty. Liberation theology is reflection based on pastoral practice, and that pastoral practice entails a lengthy process of restoring to persons through communal development and initiative the humanity of which they have been robbed. No one I have ever met who has worked in the popular organizations of Latin America has ever been tempted to idealize the poor. There is admiration for their ability to endure and to hope. But there is also a recognition, even on the part of the poor themselves, that poverty gives rise to brokenness that is difficult to overcome. Brutality, despair, distrust, lack of initiative, lack of self-respect and co-operation, and acceptance of the very models of domination that have been used against them all obstruct the attempt to form communities of integral persons among the poor. Neither liberation theology nor popular organizations are, in my opinion, the source of the romanticization of the poor, though at times in their admiration for the organized poor with whom they work, pastoral workers, among them liberation theologians, may praise "the poor" active in this neighborhood or that, without making clear to listeners that this praise is aimed at a specific group of poor people who have in years of communal struggle against poverty regained much of the dignity and humanity robbed from them by endemic poverty. They know this, and they say it often—but perhaps not often enough to make clear to their popularizers. It is these popularizers of, and the audience for, liberation theology—people from the First World, or friends from other social classes—who romanticize the poor. Perhaps they merely misunderstand. Perhaps they are motivated by feelings of guilt or complicity, perhaps by an unwillingness to recognize, through identifying with the brokenness of the poor, their own need to be healed. Some are motivated by a strong need for hope, for a certainty that liberation *will* occur, that their efforts are not in vain, and thus idealize the poor as the inevitable liberators of us all.

DANGERS IN ROMANTICIZING THE POOR

This romanticization of the poor is just as dangerous to the cause of the poor as the church's earlier legitimation of poverty through romanticization. When we romanticize the victims of social oppression and ignore their brokenness, their need for conversion, we set them up. We act as if, given the end of the particular tyranny which began their cycle of oppression, they will be self-sufficient, can be leaders, can protect their own interests. This is the problem with liberal approaches to exploitation. What ties classic liberals—libertarians—to contemporary liberals is the assumption that social harmony occurs through the interaction of competing social groups representing their own self-interests. Libertarians argue that to have this occur government must not restrain any economic factors; contemporary liberals argue that for all groups to engage in this process government must intervene to unchain previously exploited groups through, for example, ensuring civil rights for blacks, freedom of activity for labor unions, and preventing discrimination against women and minorities. But competition based on self-interest inevitably oppresses some groups and individuals; in a system with such a premise, contemporary liberals will always be unchaining past victims for new ones are always being created.

The effects of victimization live on after the chains. Modern revolutions since the French Revolution often begin by proclaiming their cause to be that of the poor. But because there is not sufficient attention to the consequences of poverty which handicap the poor from organizing, communicating their goals and objectives, or raising sufficient leaders from their ranks, once the former structure is overcome and the task of creating a new reality begins, leadership of the revolution often passes to the non-poor. When we idealize the poor we make their real liberation more improbable, for we fail to provide for their real needs through social empowerment.

Yet there is still another way that romanticizing victims endangers those very victims. When any group of victims, such as the poor, fail to live up to their idealized image, disillusion creeps over their allies, and a backlash against the poor sets in, jeopardizing all they struggled for. How often do individuals or groups from the middle class, inspired by romantic understandings of the poor, begin programs in social work, community organizing or international development work, only to be "burnt out" and adopt reactionary politics out of dismay at the difficulty of organizing the poor, at their resistance to change, and at the brutality and inertia among the poor? Romanticizing the poor sets the stage for new forms of manipulation of the poor and inevitably strengthens the oppressive structures that control them.

At the other extreme, romanticization of the poor by would-be allies can also lead to extremist violence by the left. I am not here advancing a pacifist argument against any leftist recourse to violence, but only insisting that recourse to violence should be limited to situations where it can defend and not further weaken justice, and where there are no workable alternatives. Recourse to violence in place of organizing and education of the poor is morally indefensible, largely because it is not ultimately effective.

If the cause of the poor is just but seems blocked by the intransigence of the elites, romanticization of the poor can lead to an easy adoption of violence as the path to justice. For if the poor are idealized, if we have absolved them of sin because of the justness of their cause, then we do not need to worry that they may be carried away by violence, by the desire for revenge. We do not need to fear that their anger may not be channeled well, or that the poor have learned their attitudes toward violence from those who have treated them with violence and without dignity.

Many times we find among the leadership corps of terrorist movements individuals who made the cause of some marginated group their own despite a background of relative privilege. Such individuals often turned to violence after finding other less extreme paths slow and obstructed. They do not have much experience at waiting, and are uncomfortable feeling responsible to those oppressed persons for the lack of improvement in their lives. From their point of view, how can they accept delay when it means the further deaths of children from malnutrition, or an increase in the numbers of the assassinated and disappeared? Worse, how can they expect those directly affected to accept such delays in liberation? This is an understandable attitude. But it is only when we fail to see the oppressed as they are, as unjustly violated and yet nevertheless partially deformed or dehumanized by acceptance of that unjust violation, that we can idealize them as both uncorrupted by the violence in their past, and incorruptible by the violence now advocated.

RECENT EXAMPLES OF ROMANTICIZING THE POOR

Contemporary romanticization of the poor—especially of the far distant poor—is not only an abstract, theological romanticization of the poor but is readily visible in contemporary politics. I have been struck by four distinct examples in the United States these last few years. The first concerns martyrdom. If there is any theme in Latin American liberation theology which gets through to college or parish audiences in the United States it is martyrdom. My experience as a teacher is that anyone who has ever read, for example, Penny Lernoux's account of the church's struggle to defend human rights in Latin America in the sixties and seventies[19] comes away virtually convinced by the tales of martyrdom alone of the truth of liberation theology.

I have sensed a morbid love of blood in much interest in liberation theology, which for some sets the limits on their interest in justice. For there is a corresponding decline of interest when I explain to classes and church groups that in the eighties the overall number of deaths and cases of torture went down significantly after many countries returned to civilian rule. It is assumed that the truth of the theology is directly proportional to the numbers of its dead and tortured, and that a change from military to civilian rule is automatically a move from unjust social system to just social system. If the number of murders declines from 10,000 to 5000 and there are no dead priests for awhile, presumably Christ has moved on to areas more bloodsoaked.

Such an approach benefits the systems of domination. A few years ago, the U.S. State Department insisted that the human-rights record of the government of El Salvador was much improved since death squad activity went down, that the innocent were not being killed in such numbers as before. But the archdiocese of San Salvador pointed out that total deaths of civilians were not down at all. The government had merely shifted to a strategy of first designating large areas of the country "free fire" zones in which any life was assumed to be an enemy, and then using helicopter gunships to kill any warm body detected by the infrared sensors, whether it be old men, women, children, or livestock. These were called war casualties, instead of assassinations, and were not understood by many in congress to be human-rights abuses.

Judging the righteousness and urgency of a cause by the numbers of its dead, or the categories into which the dead are placed, merely encourages more subtle methods of death and repression, such as the hundreds of thousands of Latin American "disappearances." In order to inhibit groundswells of sympathy and support for massive numbers of victims, repressive governments often shift from open assassination to more subtle forms of oppression. During the time lapse required to understand the new forms and inform potential critics of the system, momentum against such systems is lost. When we focus on the numbers of dead as our criterion for locating injustice, we leave ourselves open to manipulation.

Our moral concern regarding socio-political systems should hinge on the dignity, well-being, equality, and participation assured to all members of society. When we allow our concern to hinge on proof of massive numbers of innocent dead by violent atrocities, we play into the hands of perpetrators of injustice. The point of martyrdom is not that some few are better, different or designated for greatness, but rather that ordinary people with feet of clay—like us—can persevere in love despite the threat of suffering and death.

Some U.S. supporters of the former Sandinista government in Nicaragua are a second example of romanticizing victims, and some supporters of the sanctuary movement for Salvadoreans and Guatemalans are a third. Now hear me clearly. I have fully supported both of these movements as necessary social-justice actions. But those who in support of these have ignored or denied injustices done by the Sandinistas, or insisted on the prior noninvolvement of all the refugees in violence, were setting up these movements for ultimate failure.

If U.S. foreign policy is to improve toward nations like Sandinista-Nicaragua or any other revolutionary state, it must incorporate not only respect for the autonomy of other nations, but also a consistent method for assessing both the interests of the people of that nation as well as the those of the United States before making aid determinations. What was wrong with the U.S. policy of boycott and *contra* support was that it applied to Nicaragua demanding standards of justice which were not applied to any other Latin nation (and could not be met by any other nation) and that it violated Nicaraguan political autonomy in ways we would never permit any of our allies' (or our own) autonomy to be violated. (In this, of course, United States treatment of Nicaragua was not singular. The United States invaded Panama for the purpose of capturing General Noriega for trial in U.S. courts, though no U.S. citizen would grant any other nation the right to invade the U.S. in order to capture President Bush for trial on violating that nation's laws.)

Persons who felt the need to defend Nicaragua by assuming that, because the government significantly improved the situation of the poor, it was therefore incapable of wrongdoing, did Nicaragua no favors. I heard support for the Sandinistas from the religious left in the United States which included arguments for the absolute necessity of Sandinista press censorship (in a nation where the Sandinistas had just won almost three quarters of the votes?), excuses for inciting and organizing mobs to assault political opposition, dismissal of the serious early grievances of Miskito Indians, and justification for seizing, contrary to Sandinista laws, the land of members of the political opposition (land which was being effectively farmed). The Sandinistas were not totally sinless, even if the level of their offenses did not compare to that of other Latin governments. Excusing their wrongdoings did nothing to encourage them to move toward a more rigorous justice, and it provided invaluable ammunition to supporters of U.S. policy, who argued for ignoring the U.S. religious left because it had been brainwashed by clever marxists in Managua during ten day government-planned bus tours.

To a similar extent, the sanctuary movement has among its popularizers some who, recognizing the unjust and inhumane slaughter of the civilian population in Salvador and Guatemala and the need to grant sanctuary here, assume that the victims of the military death machines are, because they are victims, innocent civilians. Sanctuary workers have often been in a double bind, for the welfare and ultimate safety of individual refugees often demands silence about refugees' earlier political activities, while this same silence can support the very injustice which creates refugees.

Claims of innocence are problematic, for they ignore the ability of evil, of violence, to provoke both violence and evil. There are many "total innocents" among the refugees, in the sense of those uninvolved in the struggle. But besides these bystanders drawn into the struggle of others there are many forced to flee because they chose counterviolence or support for counterviolence as a response to the tremendous structural injustice in their country and to the massive repressive violence which maintains it. This is legitimate; I am not arguing that such people are wrong, or that they do not deserve sanctuary unless they are non-partisan and nonviolent. But presenting all refugees as "innocent" bystanders in a violent civil war, though it may help arouse the sympathy of many, only strengthens the hand of the right wing in the end by implying that those who are involved in the violence on either side are equally "guilty." This makes it possible to justify U.S. support for one of the guilty sides on the grounds of either national interest, or often, anticommunism.

The sanctuary movement in the United States must be primarily directed not to changing U.S. immigration policy on asylum (though that is a worthy secondary goal) but to changing U.S. foreign policy so that this country is not collaborating in the creation of refugees who need sanctuary. Only a small percentage of the Central American refugees of state violence reach refuge in the United States, and few of these can obtain legal asylum. While sanctuary workers should not endanger the chances of individual refugees for asylum should they be arrested by the Immigration and Naturalization Service (INS) they cannot make the case for the need for sanctuary based on the nonpartisanship of refugees in general. To have been involved in the struggle for justice should not disqualify one for humanitarian relief once the battlefield is left behind. But so long as appeals for concern are based on the noninvolvement of refugees in armed struggle and not on the injustice of the political situation from which they flee, U.S. policy in Salvador is not challenged by the sanctuary movement.

VICTIMS AND INNOCENCE

There are, of course, historical reasons why this insistence on seeing refugees as noninvolved bystanders is a tempting trap. In historical discussions of war, pacifists assume that all violence is evil and corrupting of those who use it,[20] and just war theorists assume that noncombatants are innocent and should be spared violence which can be legitimately inflicted on combatants.[21] Both introduce an identification of noncombatants with "innocence" which, if uncritically accepted, can lead to assumptions that all combatants are somehow guilty. In the situation from which these refugees flee, injustice arises from both the social structures which military violence defends and from the repressive methods by which the military defends those structures. The counterviolence is not equally guilty, but it, too, is sometimes corrupted by the evil in the situation, and is tempted into actions of revenge.

A contemporary example of this division of innocent and guilty based on use of violence is the work of Amnesty International, which agitates for the release and humane treatment of all political prisoners who have never had recourse to violence.[22] With great regret, Amnesty International limits its work to nonviolent political prisoners only because more can be done immediately for this huge group by distinguishing them from cases where more complex evaluations of the justice of violence and counterviolence are required. Yet the fact is that if we want to implement justice, we cannot only support the totally "innocent"—where there are any—but must make complex choices of comparative justice, while using our support to root out the lesser evils in our own group and our allies.

My fourth example concerns the more recent war in the Persian Gulf. So deeply has the romanticization of victims been embedded in our political consciousness that most of the religious left in the United States was paralysed in the recent Gulf War. So accustomed are we to the idea that we must support whatever side claims the victims that the obvious fact that many Kuwaitis were victims of a vicious invasion left much of the religious left unable to ask the necessary critical questions as to the most appropriate, just and compassionate means of ending that occupation. During a month while the United States rained the heaviest aerial bombing ever seen in war on the cities of Iraq, few voices in the United States were raised to defend the rights of innocent Iraqi civilians being victimized. Furthermore, few objected to either the military media censorship or to the voluntary media censorship which together prevented the U.S. public from confronting the extent and degree of victimization from the bombing among Iraqi civilians. Presumably, once we have located a group of victims, we know which side is right, and need not be alert to the creation of others.

The romanticization of victims is not only dangerous because it prevents so many from looking beyond the suffering of these victims. The tendency of the populace to romanticize victims, and to focus on those victims to the exclusion of all other considerations, including the potential for future victimization, gives to the media enormous power, in that the media (or the media and the government) decides which victims will be revealed to us. The media, and especially TV, thus have the power to decide for most of us which victims we will support and which we will ignore or oppose, even to the extent of war. Given the fact that a good part of the peoples of the world live in some kind of state of victimization, this power of the media is terrifying. We are only now beginning to hear the horror stories from

Iraq, and those stories are dominated by focus on the plight of the Kurds, who fear ongoing Iraqi reprisals. There is little in the news to raise questions about the beautifully precise surgical bombing of military targets in Iraq, despite the fact that the majority of the more than 130,000 Iraqi dead were civilians. Perhaps such news will come later, as did the reports of the mass graves of 3000–5000 poor Panamanians killed in the U.S. invasion and secretly buried before reporters were allowed into Panama, which took more than a year to reach the *Congressional Record*, and thus some of the nation's news media. In the meantime, of course, our nation is compiling a series of wins in what are called "bloodless little wars." Until the religious left learns to move beyond emotional responses to bloody victims, to insist on obtaining the entire picture in all its structural complexity, it will be open to manipulation.

DEATH/RESURRECTION: PROBLEM PARADIGM

I believe we need to consider the possibility that one reason for the Christian temptation to glorify victims, death, and suffering lies not in misunderstandings of the death/resurrection paradigm for life, but in making death/resurrection the central, and perhaps only, paradigm for life.

In the last decade we have seen, especially in the feminist movement, a rejection of equations of sacrificial suffering and love, and an insistence on the merely instrumental value of sacrificial suffering: that it is good not in itself but only when its object is mutual love. Likewise in Latin American liberation theology, there is great reverence for the sacrifices of their martyrs, but an insistance that martyrdom cannot be sought, for death and suffering are not good in themselves.

We are beginning to move away from demonic understandings of the gospel in which Jesus suffered and died because that was the way in which God demanded/arranged that we be restored to life in the aftermath of the Fall. Jon Sobrino has pointed out well how we lose the meaning of Jesus when we hurry over the scandal of the cross and concentrate on resurrection.[23] This is one way to romanticize suffering and death—as mere preliminaries to resurrection—and is the distortion most common in our history of romanticizing victims.

One of the ways we distort the meaning of the cross today is to assume that when the modern Romans are defeated, that the kingdom is assured, the victims are freed, the struggle is over. But this is precisely where Jesus disagreed with the revolutionaries of his day: the coming of the reign of God demanded more than just the removal of the material forces of oppression. It demanded the transformation of all hearts, attitudes, and relationships as well, for without such transformation, the poor, the public sinners, and other unfortunates would merely be exploited and excluded by a new group of powerful people. The zealots of Jesus' day were as blind as the lepers who were healed and failed to return to Jesus—they were satisfied with too little. All those victimized by domination require a liberation which includes within the material liberation an extended process of spiritual transformation.

We need to consider the possibility that the root of our Christian temptation to glorify victims, death, and suffering lies not in such misunderstandings of the death/resurrection paradigm for life, but in making death/resurrection the central—and perhaps only—paradigm for life. Part of the failure to take seriously the effect of the cross, and to look for instantaneous resurrection comes from understanding the gospel to say that real life is resurrection, and comes after suffering and death. This is the christolatry of Christianity that is criticized by Tom Driver and Paul Knitter.[24]

Equation of real life and resurrection is, I think, an extremely common Christian assumption. But it is certainly dangerous—and also cruel—to assume that suffering inevitably leads to real life, to joy, to meaning, to wholeness. For suffering destroys. It kills, it maims the body and the spirit, it produces despair and evil. The history of human life is filled with the screams and moans of millions who have died of slow starvation, of virulent epidemics, in the massacres of wars and invasions, and at the hands of torturers and executioners. What life has been produced by such suffering? What good came of the Black Death, the witch hunts, the Holocaust, the genocide of North Amerindians? History continues to demonstrate that if there is a lesson to be learned from suffering, it is that many violated persons become violent, that those treated inhumanely often become inhumane, and that some, when left without hope, kill themselves in despair. Suffering both kills and deforms. The message of the gospel is a hope-filled response to this truth—not a negation of it.

It is also wrong to interpret the gospel to mean that real life, joy, and kingdom can only emerge from suffering (regardless of what else may result from suffering). Life is not ultimately synonymous with resurrection. We know many goods, many joys, many experiences of growth that are born naturally into our lives, not resurrected. Many of these have emerged not from death and suffering, but from love and friendship, from creative work, and from interaction with nature. Life is born—and life is good. We must lift up the goodness of life, that which Jesus attempted to demonstrate; it is good for all to eat and drink together, to bake and fish, to sow and harvest, to celebrate weddings, to cherish children, to pray, and to do these things together, without judgment or exclusion. I first came to see this not from my reading of scripture, but from observing the Latin American liberation movement and its understanding of the gospel. That movement has more than its share of martyrs, of death/resurrection experiences, and those involved are clear that the movement is fed by its martyrs. But at the same time, those people seem to be sure that the center of what their loving God wants for them is work and prayer, food and dignity, family and community—life.

We should not reject the death/resurrection motif. It is an invaluable part of our experience. There is great evil in the world, and sometimes it does overpower us regardless of our struggle. Death/resurrection is for the worst case scenario, when everything else is failed, and suffering or death is unavoidable. Then the death/resurrection motif reminds us that still there is hope. We all need this message for the rough times; for some it is the only source of hope. Once we have come through an experience of resurrection beyond death and pain, that resurrection paradigm is validated and takes on new power. Because the personal discovery of death/resurrection is so dramatic, so overwhelming, it tends to easily overshadow the value of life in its natural forms.

But if we do not insist that the center of the gospel is about birth, about natural life, and that this is the cause in which we may lose and yet find hope and life beyond suffering, then we will always be tempted to the love of death, to the glorification of victims. We cannot continue to oppose the natural good, represented by birth, with the "religious" good, represented by resurrection. I think this is the real tension in the insistence that Christianity is not a natural religion, but a historical religion. This distinction is merely another way of playing out body/soul dualism. Body/soul dualism repeatedly takes this form today in Western society; persons who are distanced from suffering, including their own, and who fear death, especially their own, are morbidly attracted to theologies of death/resurrection. Until we learn to love and to live life more fully, we cannot properly appreciate death/resurrection.

We do not have to abandon the message of Jesus' life to heed the message in his death. His death did not nullify the hope, the commitment to life, in his ministry. For the message in the death of Jesus is not that death and suffering *always* overwhelm human efforts at maximizing the goodness of life. If that were true, then the person Jesus who undertook a mission was totally mistaken, totally a failure in his life work and only the action of God in resurrecting him gives us hope—a hope for life *after* death. Rather, the message of Jesus' life *and* death is that we are called to pursue life, and even if (not when) death sometimes overwhelms us, even that death can and must be turned to the service of life. God's presence is experienced by victims of evil and suffering as the basis of hope. That hope emerges from a dialectic between concrete causes for despair and fragile but real possibilities for good in human life. In this dialectic we come to understand our participation in larger liberating processes which offer hope despite the possibility that any particular process may be aborted in the unfolding of history.

The persecuted early Christians of the book of Revelation and 1 Peter anticipated with relish the myriad sufferings and forms of death which would be visited upon their persecutors at the Second Coming Revelation, 6:7–8, 12–17; 7:6; 8:7–12; 15:1 and 2 Peter, 2:4–10, 17–21; 3:7–10. When they prayed, "Come Lord Jesus," it was at least partly out of lust for destruction and vengeance. Catherine Keller is right to point out that this same response to persecution is found today in many fundamentalist Christians who read Revelation's account of the fires, earthquakes, plagues, and of the multitudes who will beg for the release of death, and then look forward to nuclear annihilation as "God's way" to usher in the Second Coming and the completion of kingdom.[25] For these people the gospel with death/resurrection at its center legitimates a cosmic death wish for humanity, and allows revenge in the name of God. Beside this romanticization of death even the romanticization of victims looks benign. And yet they share, I believe, the same root—the centralization of death/resurrection rather than birth/life as the Christian paradigm.

CHAPTER 4

PRUDENCE AND VICTIM-BLAMING

Victim-blaming in our world takes many forms. One of the most consistent types of victim-blaming relies on accusing victims of lacking prudence. Rape victims are accused of being responsible for their rapes on the grounds that they lacked sufficient prudence when they ventured outdoors alone, accepted a date with casual acquaintances, lived alone, or failed to buy the latest word in security systems. Battery victims are accused of having lacked prudence: they must have said or done something grievous to trigger violence in their fathers, husbands, lovers, or even casual acquaintances.

In the name of prudence we caution each other not to pick up hitchhikers, take in homeless people, or render emergency medical assistance to strangers. And those who persist in such behavior and suffer robbery, rape, assault or legal suit, are assumed to have asked for what they got by violating the norm of prudence.

One particular situation in which victims are consistently blamed is social movements of disadvantaged and repressed groups. These groups are accused of imprudence when their movements produce unprovoked violence by their oppressors. They are blamed for having aroused the fear and threat which leads to the deaths of their supporters and the repression of their movement.

The centrality of the cross in Christian thought should make victim-blaming highly suspect for Christians. It would be, after all, extremely easy to make the case that Jesus asked for what he got: he publicly disparaged the rich and powerful, the Temple officials, and the scribes and Pharisees. He continued to act in ways that he knew outraged powerful people and groups, as when he continued to heal on the Sabbath (Luke 13:10–17 and 14:1–6). But Christians understand

Jesus as not only innocent, in the sense of without guilt, but also as representing divine goodness itself. It is important that Christians probe this question of if, and when, victim-blaming can ever be legitimate, since we know from the cross that not all victims are blameworthy.

VICTIM-BLAMING: LATIN AMERICA

Peru

At the beginning of 1989 the Christian left in Peru, like the left in general, was still being hit with assassinations by right-wing death squads like Rodrigo Franco, and was increasingly a target for assassinations and bombings of development projects by the extreme left terrorist movement, Sendero Luminoso. Sendero targets all parts of the political spectrum, but began to hit the left, including the left associated with the church, harder as it had become clear that the left should control the provincial elections in fall 1989 and the national elections in spring 1990. Within the Catholic church the Christian leftists were also under pressure from an increasingly conservative bishops' conference, and from continuing Vatican harassment of leading figures such as Gustavo Gutiérrez, who has served as the mentor to most of the members of the Christian left.

The Christian left was a part of an association of leftist parties and individuals ranging from moderately to very leftist, cooperating as the Izquierda Unita. The expectation that the left would be electorally victorious was based on an analysis of national elections since 1980, when a longstanding military government gave way to civilian rule under the rightist party, Accion Popular. Since then the two major issues had been the rise of Sendero, which moved from a movement localized in the Andean province of Ayacucho to a national movement well supplied with both arms and funds,[1] and the economic disaster in which Peru has been mired. In the 1985 elections, the right Accion Popular was so discredited by their failure on both economic and counterinsurgency fronts that they polled only seven percent of the vote. Since 1985, under the rule of the centrist Alianza Popular Revolucionario Americana (APRA) government of Alan Garcia, things went from bad to worse on both fronts. Garcia tried to resign in favor of the military twice, but the military did not want responsibility for the economic crisis, and was divided over Sendero. In fact, in the fall 1989 provincial elections, APRA barely carried any offices in its traditional strongholds, and none outside.

A split in the Izquierda Unita (IU) threatened from the beginning of 1989, following an IU congress held in December 1988, which finally opposed the platform of the assumed presidential candidate for the national election, Alfonso Barrantes, and established a directorate which included members of parties Barrantes had not wanted included in the IU slate.[2] By mid 1989 there was a very real split in the IU, the terrorism of Sendero continued to accelerate, and the annual inflation rate was running at 5000 percent. Within the Christian left, there were few signs of hope. The split in the IU effectively eliminated hopes of electoral victory and any meaningful structural change in the direction of relief for the majority poor; in the 1990 elections a previously unknown independent with a very unclear platform, Alberto Fujimori, was elected by a majority of Peruvians disgusted with politicians and parties in general. Church sponsored development projects, especially in the Andes, were closed down and personnel withdrawn to safety out of fear of further violence from Sendero, and the hopes of many of the poor for change through the electoral process completely evaporated in the wake of Fujimori's austerity plan, which raised prices, but not wages, 700 percent in the first five months.

Many in the Christian left took this state of affairs, and the resignation of the poor to it, as a personal failure, since their own work with the poor through the church had pressed the poor to organize so as to effect change through the electoral process. At great sacrifice, many of the poor had organized, as the amazing process of the IU Congress demonstrated, and had accepted the sacrifices and risks as Sendero assassinated their party leaders and elected officials. Now it seemed to be for nothing, and many of the poor became convinced that, regardless of its methods, Sendero appeared to be the only real hope for radical change on the horizon.

At the same time that members of the Christian left were attending the funerals of their assassinated colleagues, receiving death threats themselves, doing what they could to alleviate the horrendous increase in tuberculosis, malnutrition, and starvation among the poor with whom they work, and agonizing over the increasing resignation of the poor to the violent momentum of Sendero, they were increasingly, and still are, being blamed for the national catastrophe by a variety of sources. The basis of the charge seems to be that through their support for liberation theology and the organization of the poor they raised impossible hopes for change which led inevitably to the rise of Sendero, to counterviolence by the military and right-wing death squads, and to paralysis of the governmental system. For the Peruvian right and center, for a large part of the institutional Catholic church, and for the representatives of U.S. foreign policy in Peru, the problem of violence is the responsibility of liberation theology and its proponents, prominent among which are the members of the Christian left. They are the agitators who fed hopes of a better life to the poor. If those hopes had not been raised, the dashing of those hopes over the last decade would not have fueled the anger and violence of the poor, or the counterviolence of those threatened by their hopes, which together, it is charged, made it impossible for the Peruvian governments of the 1980s and 1990s to avoid the total economic collapse in which Peru exists today.

El Salvador

Similarly in El Salvador, there has been a full scale terror campaign against the churches involved in defense of the human rights of the poor. The 1989 assassination of the six Jesuit priests and two women at the Central American University are well-known. But this was not an isolated event. Within the same period of a few weeks at the end of 1989, a contingent of visiting Canadian Lutherans were arrested and interrogated for information about the location of Lutheran Bishop Medardo Gomez, who has become the new Oscar Romero of El Salvador. A contingent of Salvadorean Episcopal church workers were arrested and tortured until one gave the location of the Reverend Luis Serrano, ranking Episcopal priest in El Salvador, who was then arrested. Hundreds of Salvadorean church workers were arrested within this same period, including a handful of foreigners who engage in refugee or education work. Besides their church membership and activity, what tied all these people together is their concern for human rights, for the right of all Salvadoreans to life without torture, assassination, or detention without trial.

Response to these killings, tortures, and arrests in the United States ranged from a characterization of these events as deplorable but understandable, as excesses by a government fighting communist insurgency, to charges that the church workers were either rebels or dupes of the rebels, who knew the risks of their activities. Some U.S. congressmen and senators, responding to the demands of sympathetic church people in the United States that it cut off its $1.4 million/ day support for the Salvadorean military, took the position that the government remains the moderate party between the Frente Farabundo Martí para la Liberación Nacional (FMLN) and the death squads. They reason that if only more Salvadoreans (including those who were killed, tortured and arrested) had supported the government more strongly—that is, not condemned the military's human-rights violations—such violence would not have occurred, because the guerillas would not have moved their campaign to San Salvador, thus provoking army attacks on critics of the government.[3] Thus the ones really guilty of the killings are the victims themselves, whose imprudence cost them their lives.

The conclusions of *Santa Fe II: A Strategy for Latin America in the 90's,*[4] a document of the Inter-American Security Educational Institute, whose *Santa Fe I* produced the Reagan agenda for Latin America in the eighties, as well as Latin American diplomatic posts for its authors, is relevant here. *Santa Fe II* characterizes liberation theology as a "political doctrine disguised as religious belief, having an anti-papal and anti-free enterprise meaning, in order to weaken society's independence from statist control."[5] Because it so understands liberation theology, its treatment of human rights is repressive: "The U.S. should recognize the need of governments attempting to create democratic regimes to restrain anti-democratic parties . . . It should also differentiate between human rights groups which sustain the democratic regime from those which support statism."[6] Are we to understand that the present ruling party in Salvador, begun by the instigator of both the death squads in general and the murder of Archbishop Romero, which through President Cristiani commands the troops that arrested all the church people and killed the Jesuits, is an example of a government "attempting to create [a] democratic regime(s)?" Such a characterization of liberation theology and of human rights amounts to war on at least large sectors of mainstream Christianity in Latin America. If the agenda of the Peruvian left to reorganize the economy is an example of statism, does this mean that the United States is urging the Peruvian government to see the Christian democratic left as synonymous with Sendero, and to accord similar treatment to their adherents? What then distinguishes a democratic regime from a statist one if not equal protection of all who live within the law from abuse and death by the state? Is disagreement with the policies of one's government through lawful means sufficiently imprudent to justify the loss of one's life or freedom?

VICTIM-BLAMING: UNITED STATES

Such examples are not restricted to other nations. In Taylor Branch's splendid account of the early civil rights movement in the United States, *Parting the Waters: America During the King Years, 1954–*

1963[7] he detailed again and again the anguish among civil rights leaders caused by the stance of the Eisenhower and Kennedy administrations, of southern governors and judges (even liberals), of the newspaper and TV reporters, and consequently by much of the nation at large, that it was the responsibility of the civil rights leaders to see that blacks—both protesters and bystanders—were not targeted for violence. That is, the civil rights leaders were to insure that they took no action whose tactics, goals or timing would provoke violent backlash from segregationists.

The governmental response to the Freedom Riders (urging the first group of Freedom Riders to abort the bus trip and complete their journey by plane, and, through the attorney general, attempting to stop Diane Nash and the Student Nonviolent Coordinating Committee from sending a group of replacements to Alabama)[8] demonstrated that though federal law and the federal courts had made clear that interstate buses were to be integrated, responsibility for violence done to the Freedom Riders who claimed that right to integrated interstate travel rested with the Riders themselves and with the civil rights movement which they represented.

The attempt to register blacks to vote in the South, which resulted in fires, bombings, assassinations, and beatings,[9] was similarly blamed for the resulting violence, even by some blacks.[10] The press reaction to the Birmingham campaign was that it was "of doubtful utility, poorly timed," and motivated by movement politics. The press supported the appeal of white clergy to end civil rights demonstrations in Birmingham because "such actions as incite hatred and violence, however technically peaceful those actions may be, have not contributed to the resolution of the local problems. We do not believe that extreme measures are justified in Birmingham."[11] This despite the fact that at this time King, Ralph Abernathy and fifty-two supporters were in the Birmingham jail. The argument seemed to be that the civil rights leaders knew that their opposition was dangerously and immorally violent, not to mention irrational; if they chose to provoke such people, they were responsible for the results.

Such a response presumes the relative normativity of segregation or of any similar longstanding injustice. Even many liberals, who recognized the lack of justice in the situation of the Peruvian poor, of the Salvadorean church workers, or of Southern blacks of the fifties, nevertheless treated the status quo as more or less normal, if not normative, in that the risk of possible violence in the future was presumed to be more dangerous and harmful than the continuation of the present situation of injustice which included a great deal of violence. It should be apparent that such a judgment is much easier to make when the injustice of the present is not experienced by one's own community, but by other communities. It is often easy to rationalize that such and such a group has been putting up with such treatment for many years (decades, centuries?) and they still seem relatively happy—look at how they love to sing and dance, or to celebrate their saints' festivals! So it can't be so bad, surely not bad enough to risk social violence which could get out of hand (read: could touch others, especially us).

Movements for social change are sometimes forced by circumstances into accepting some of this responsibility. Blacks heard again and again that they bore responsibility for allowing injustice to be understood as normative, in that they failed to mount large scale protest in the past, so that segregationists could claim that segregation was acceptable to both sides until this handful of radicals began agitating. When blacks did challenge the segregated system, they were accused of provoking violence, and they felt they had to accept responsibility for resulting violence, for two reasons. The first and more pragmatic reason for accepting responsibility for provoking the violence of segregationsts was that the civil rights movement needed the financial and political support of others, and therefore was dependent upon its image as created by the press and government officials for the rest of the nation. Neither Harry Belafonte's personal efforts nor Jack O'Dell's mail solicitation for the Student Christian Leadership Conference (SCLC) would ever have been able to keep raising the bail money that kept the movement going, and sympathetic judges would have been even harder to find, had the movement been portrayed as provoking violence carelessly or deliberately, however nonviolently. Appearances were important also for getting blacks in new cities to join the movement.

A second reason for accepting responsibility for the violence of the opposition was more traditional than pragmatic: the civil rights movement was led by clergy, accustomed to seeing themselves as the shepherds of their congregations. The SCLC, as contrasted to the SNCC Freedom Riders or lunch counter demonstrators, felt responsible not only for their own lives, which many were willing to lay on the line, but for the lives of the flocks they had persuaded to join the movement. They felt obliged to ask proportionality questions: What were the risks of provoking violence? how much violence? for what gain? how certain a gain?

And yet *publicly* civil rights leaders like Martin Luther King Jr. rejected again and again the argument that the civil rights movement was responsible for the violence of segregationists. It was, he remarked, like blaming Jesus for his own crucifixion.

PRUDENCE AND PROPORTIONALISM: PROBABLE SUCCESS

How is it that such blatantly unjust victim-blaming becomes accepted by Christians? Is there any support for such a position in traditional Christian teaching? Christian ethics has been moving away from commandment morality for some decades now, insisting that religious commandments and church laws do not define ethical behavior so much as offer general guidelines based on conclusions from experience of previous Judeo-Christian communities. Moral behavior among Christians should be regulated not by absolute moral rules, but by individual consciences whose formation includes careful consideration of the inherited conclusions. Those individual consciences make moral choices using proportionalism, either alone or in combination with loyalty to inherited commandments or principles. Any use of proportionalism—estimating, then weighing the negative and positive consequences of each option, and choosing the one with the most positive outcome—will require an emphasis on prudence, on careful use of reason. While commandment morality makes little or no use of prudence in that individuals are merely required to obey the commandments, proportionalism cannot hope to accurately estimate the consequences of proposed actions without the use of prudence, and without accurate estimates of consequences it is impossible to choose the more beneficent set of consequences.

In Christian ethical tradition some issues have been generally treated through a commandment morality, such as sexuality, while others, usually more social and less personal issues, such as war, have been treated with at least a partially proportional method necessitating prudence. While some criteria of the Christian just war theory are not based on proportional weighing, but are given as absolute commands (the requirements for noncombatant immunity, or for competent authority, for example) others are clearly proportional—in fact, proportionality itself is both a criteria for declaring just war (*jus ad bellum*), and for waging just war (*jus in bello*). But the proportional criteria in just war theory which most closely approximates the form of prudence which victims are accused of neglecting is the probable success requirement of just war theory.

Within just war theory, the only moral justification for the violence and destruction of war is redress of serious injustices not open to alternative means of redress. Thus, if war is unable to redress the grievance, war should not be declared. The probable success requirement insists that preservation of life and minimization of destruction take precedence over a right to heroic, patriotic, violent national defense, as this has historically been expressed in futile, self-sacrificial wars. It is important to remember, however, that forbidding the declaration of wars which cannot be won does not mandate acceptance of injustice of the strong over the weak. Other methods of collective resistance to injustice remain open. Furthermore, history is full of the victories of dwarfs over giants, including the American Revolution, the American defeat in Vietnam, and the Soviet defeat in Afghanistan. Given certain conditions, the weak can sometimes justifiably predict probable success.

If the probable success requirement in just war theory bans initiating a situation—war—in which violence occurs without real possibilities for restoring/creating justice, then perhaps there is precedent here for barring initiation of other situations in which violence results from vain attempts at justice. Is this form of prudence—the requirement for probable success—the root of the common condemnation of social-justice movements whose protests provoke widespread violence from their opposition? Can such an understanding of prudence—requiring probable success before initiating movements for justice—be legitimately used to limit evangelization efforts? That is, can prudence be used to prevent evangelization efforts, such as those of the SCLC, liberation theology, and human-rights proponents in Latin America, efforts which present the liberation of their victims from social, economic, and political oppression as the will of God and therefore an obligation for Christians? When it is likely that non-violent, even legal liberation efforts by victims will provoke widespread violence, does prudence require that evangelization be restricted to presenting liberation as a gradual possibility, or even an eschatological reality?

EVANGELIZATION AND INJUSTICE

Evangelization is, quite literally, the spreading of the good news, the news of the ministry, death, and resurrection of Jesus Christ with all its significance for human life. Though sometimes understood as the literal telling of the gospel and its formal acceptance by hearers, increasingly Christians of many churches have come to view evangelization as ꞌore than augmenting the numbers who bow down at the name of Jesus. Rather, evangelization is coming to be understood as the humanization of the world, the creation of societies in which all individuals become more like Jesus Christ's model of the divinely-perfect human being. True evangelization focuses on the understanding that the gospel of Jesus Christ is not completed, but paradigmatic: we are called to ministry like that of Jesus, and in that ministry we risk suffering and even death, with hope for the vindication which Jesus' resurrection promises.

Evangelization is a process which begins with an experience of the gratuitous love of God, an experience usually mediated through other humans.[12] The experience of God's gratuitous love frees human beings: it gives us a sense of our own worth and dignity, and frees us to express that worth and dignity through loving others. We grow through the love relationships we establish with God and other persons and we act together with others against conditions and situations which threaten our individual and collective new-found dignity and worth, understanding such threats as sinful, as attacks on the new persons created out of God's love.

Segundo Galilea writes: "The basic challenge of evangelization is the challenge of Christian hope . . . Evangelization is the following of Christ the Evangelizer and cooperation with him in his evangelization practice, or it is nothing."[13] Evangelization thus has very real social expressions. If evangelization has brought us to feel loved and valuable, and to respond with love for God, ourselves, and others, then we cannot sit idle when we, or others in our community, are treated as less than human, as objects having no intrinsic value. To sit idle is to accept the risk that such treatment wears down the self-respect, the hope and the agency of its victims. This would be to erode real belief in the resurrection, to accept the suffering and death of the crucifixion as final.

Such an understanding of evangelization as necessitating social action is not limited to liberation theologians. Even the Vatican Congregation for the Doctrine of the Faith in the midst of its campaign against the theology of liberation for reducing the gospel to liberation from unjust social structures, said in its "Instructions on Christian Freedom and Liberation:"

> Evangelization and the vocation to be children of God, to which all are called, have as a consequence the direct and imperative requirement of respect for all human beings in their rights to life and to dignity. There is no gap between love of neighbor and desire for justice. To con-

trast the two is to distort both love and justice. . . . The evil inequalities and oppression of every kind which afflict millions of men and women today openly contradict Christ's Gospel and cannot leave the conscience of any Christian indifferent.

The Church in her docility to the Spirit goes forward faithfully along paths to authentic liberation. Her members are aware of their failings and their delays in this quest. But a vast number of Christians, from the time of the apostles onward, have committed their powers and their lives to liberation from every form of oppression and the promotion of human dignity. The experience of the saints and the examples of so many works of service to one's neighbor are an incentive and a beacon for the liberating undertakings that are needed today.[14]

Throughout history, the demands of such evangelization fall hardest on the weak, whose very weakness makes the risks involved in service much more dangerous. In the United States, the black church has been a principal resource of blacks facing centuries of slavery, repression, and discrimination. The black churches taught the gospel and insisted on God's love for and eventual liberation of God's captive people. Nevertheless, generations of black parents, faced with frequent violence by whites determined to preserve black subordination to whites in the South even after the Civil War, felt forced to, and forced to raise their children to, accept humiliation and degradation meekly in order to survive. Such training was especially destructive for boys because they were also subjected to social conditioning that real men did not accept such treatment. The hundreds of young black men lynched, shot, or beaten to death for offending the inflated egos of their would-be masters confirmed for many black parents the wisdom of their choice: better less a man than no man at all. The nationally publicized murder of fourteen-year-old Emmett Till in Mississippi in 1955 for flirting with a white store clerk demonstrated not only continued white willingness to kill assertive black youth, but also the willingness of the legal system to condone such behavior. While this enraged much of the black population, it also confirmed for many blacks the need to teach their children meekness to white authority.

In the popular novel by Alice Walker, *The Color Purple*, Alfonso explains to his stepdaughter Celie that her father and uncle were lynched for having a store which competed with white stores too successfully. He then details how he managed to survive in a similar situation:

> The trouble with our people is that as soon as they got out of slavery they didn't want to give the white man nothing else. But the fact is, you got to give 'em something. Either your money, your land, your woman

or your ass. So what I did was just right off to offer to give 'em money. Before I planted a seed, I made sure this one and that one knowed one seed out of three was planted for him. Before I ground a grain of wheat, the same thing. And when I opened up your Daddy's old store in town I bought me my own white boy to run it. And what made it so good . . . I bought him with white folks' money."[15]

It is difficult to criticize those who adopted such survival techniques, or taught them to their children. At the same time, such survival techniques are not readily compatible with evangelization, for the victims over time are tempted to use other victims as they have been used, as Alfonso did to Celie. If in some situations complicity with evil is the only alternative to martyrdom from remaining true to one's dignity and love, then evangelization can offer a very difficult choice indeed.

MARTYRDOM

This brings us to the question of martyrdom. In the contemporary world, the Latin American church has probably reflected more on the concept of martyrdom than any other. In that reflection, in which prudence plays an important role, there is an implicit criticism of many of the early Christian martyrs who have been presented in lives of the saints as pursuing martyrdom. Reflection in Latin American churches over the last three decades has insisted that martyrdom cannot be legitimately sought. True martyrdom is the loss of one's life in Christian service to others, in defense of their lives, their dignity, and their basic human rights. Service to others is primary, and death only admirable if lost in the cause of that service. Since the loss of one's life limits one's ability to serve, service to others must always be prudently chosen. If there are ways to protect human life, dignity, and rights without endangering lives, those ways take precedence over more risky strategies. Here reflection on martyrdom and the probable success requirement are similar in insisting on the importance of prudence in attempting to preserve lives and human society. Frequently fleeing and avoiding enemies, Jesus did not pursue death, but neither did he back off from his mission of announcing and embodying God's kingdom when it risked his death and that of his followers, even when he saw no immediate victory, only betrayal and abandonment ahead.

RESISTING INJUSTICE: EVANGELICAL OBLIGATION?

Even if we can agree that individuals must be free to choose between action which leads to martyrdom and some degree of complicity in injustice, this does not resolve the issue. I can make this choice for myself; do I have the right to choose for others? It would have been morally good, though not obligatory, for Alfonso to bury Celie's lynched father in a marked grave with public rites, or to press legal authorities to investigate his death, even if Alfonso risked retaliation from whites in so doing. But would it have been morally acceptable for black ministers in the South after World War I to attempt to lead blacks by example and exhortation to respond to the gospel of love and justice by resisting white domination and degradation? Before the historical conditions which led to the costly success of the civil rights movement, would not such an evangelical demand have been a demand for mass martyrdom? Would such a crusade not have been futile before there was support from some federal courts, before television could display to the nation the vicious brutality of bombs, dogs, fire hoses, and billy clubs used against children, old women and other peaceful demonstrators? Who has the right to say to weak victims that they have an obligation to oppose even serious, blatant injustice, when that opposition will probably cost the lives of victims?

On the other hand, who has the right to say to victims that they lack the moral right to oppose serious injustice because more will probably die in vain in such opposition? Do the obligations to witness to one's faith, to evangelize others, to do justice, only exist where such witness is safe and easily successful? If so, how do we deal with the example of Jesus, who called his followers to take up their crosses and follow him? But if such obligations exist even in the face of defeat and death, then must we criticize those who refuse to witness to the full gospel when this involves being the catalyst which triggers mass visits by the angel of death?

The gospel of hope sometimes triggers reasoned, peaceful resistence or noncompliance by victims, whose oppressors then respond with mass campaigns of death and terror. Thus the nonviolent civil rights campaign triggered assassinations, bombings, and beatings by white segregationists,[16] and human-rights protests by Latin American church people began two decades of torture, disappearances, and assassinations of clergy, religious and lay church workers among the Latin American poor.[17] We often apply the probable success requirement of just war theory to armed revolutions aimed at ending massive injustice. Should we assume a similar principle banning nonviolent direct action aimed at justice when it will likely trigger massive violence by the oppressors? Such a ban differs from the probable success requirement in just war because probable success can prevent the weak from beginning a war in the cause of justice, but leaves open other means of preserving justice. A more general ban on any activity for justice which will probably provoke the opposition to create a worse situation—as has often been proposed against the antiapartheid movement in South Africa, for example—could possibly prohibit all activity aimed at justice for the oppressed.

In a recent discussion of this argument in a meeting of ethicists it was suggested that none of us have the right to dictate the choices of others in such situations, that people must decide for themselves what is moral and ethical from within these situations. But it seems to me that this is not a sufficient answer. To invoke private conscience at this point ignores the role of the churches, who have obligations to decide what the role of social justice is in evangelization, and how ministers, priests, and lay agents of the church will be trained and supported in teaching and implementing the role of social justice in evangelization. Privatization of conscience here is an evasion of the teaching role of the church toward both ministers and laity. The churches at the very least need to provide general criteria concerning the role of social justice in evangelization which can be variously adapted and interpreted at the local level.

I suggest we begin this task by examining our understandings of prudence and its role in victim-blaming. I suspect that there are two unexamined presuppositions underlying many uses of prudence in victim-blaming. One is that death or threat of death from violence is more serious than any other evil. This is an oversimplification, and at base irreconcilable with the cross of Jesus Christ. The value of life extends beyond its physical fact. We should not then assume that efforts toward justice should automatically back down or cease upon encountering the threat of physical violence. More careful weighing is necessary.

My second suggestion regarding reflection on the understanding of prudence is that we need to reject our often unconscious presupposition that conflict, especially violence, is avoidable. This is an assumption of people who live in relative security and comfort, who take the existence of justice for granted, and assume that suffering and evil can for the most part be avoided. From such an assumption it is easy to assume that it is imprudent "agitators" and radicals who are responsible for threats to peace.

A broader perspective on the world in which we live reveals that "devil theories"—beliefs that some individuals personify evil and constitute threats to an otherwise harmonious world—are not realistic and therefore not useful for creating justice. Such theories are not only the recourse of a conservative right which struggles to preserve the status quo. Too often prudence is interpreted by those torn between the requirements of justice and fear of change to require "middle ways" between extremes. Thus southern "moderates" called for middle ways between the violent segregationists and the Negro "agitators" attempting to claim the rights bestowed on them by federal law. But justice sometimes calls for extreme changes. Interpreting prudence in terms of middle ways and gradualism often blinds us to the requirements of justice, and causes us to label the very forces calling for justice as "extremist devils."

If we examine the uses of prudence, the way we understand our world and our Christian values, I think we will move in the direction of understanding prudence as of instrumental and never ultimate value. Prudence can be useful in the achievement of justice but evangelization for justice should never be dead-ended by concerns for prudence. The gospel is risky business. Prudence should be used to minimize the risks of pursuing the fullness of the kingdom, without decreasing in any way efforts to realize it.

CHAPTER 5

SEXUAL VICTIMIZATION: BEYOND SEXUAL ABUSE

In the last decade or two we have been bombarded with information about sexual abuse. Statistics on rape, sexual abuse of children, sexual assault among prison inmates, on the institutionalized elderly and mentally ill, and sexual harassment on the job have become common newspaper fare. Most of us have been shocked to learn the prevalence of these forms of victimization. We are coming to accept that our churches bear some responsibility for supporting and maintaining such victimization not only because they have so often pastorally turned a blind eye to the plight of such victims, but because both church teachings and church structures have often, at least indirectly, supported such victimization.

Counselors who work with raped or battered women are accustomed to horror stories involving pastors and other church personnel, who, when appealed to for support by these victims, have responded not only with questions about what the victim did to provoke the attack, but also with advice that victims ask forgiveness of God, do penance, and, within marriages, forgive husbands and accept their lot as wives in hope of heavenly reward. Equally common is the pastor who wrings his hands, claims a lack of expertise in the area, and suggests the victim find someone else to talk to—leaving her feeling like a leper who might contaminate him and his flock of saints. At the pastoral level, many churches have a strong tendency to assume that such victimization does not happen to the innocent redeemed in the pews, but only to those outside the churches.[1]

Yet those who work with victims of sexual abuse also charge the churches with teachings that encourage sexual abuse. The biblical treatment of incest, of women and of children, as discussed in chapter

1, provides strong evidence supporting such a charge. The romanticization of victimization resulting from the use of the cross as the central metaphor for human life, as discussed in chapter 4, is central to the common pastoral motif of self-sacrifice as essentially Christian, which functions to resign victims to their suffering.[2] Ironically, the preaching of self-sacrifice in the churches often does not serve to make the priviledged take on some of the burdens of victims, but rather serves to increase the burdens of the victims. This occurs because the preached message about the need to take up our crosses as the way to follow Jesus leads all of us to focus on responding to the suffering already present in our lives. To a battered wife the message of self-sacrifice is easily interpreted in terms of accepting her abuse. For those spared abuse and victimization the message of self-sacrifice can be interpreted to demand resignation to the process of aging, to the death of loved ones, to the necessity of lowering career goals, to the acceptance of rigorous diet and exercise plans the doctor recommends, or to volunteering in the neighborhood school, all of which can entail suffering and self-sacrifice, but none of which relieve the burden of the most seriously victimized of our society.

The structures of our churches also affect the Christian complicity in sexual abuse. Though some Christian churches have begun to ordain women, and to allow them some participation in decision making at most levels of the church, this is by no means universal, and even where it occurs, women are a distinct minority as yet relatively powerless. Though a disproportionate number of church members are women, the churches present a masculine leadership face. This fact gives support to social concepts of women's subordination and necessary control by men, which, in turn, set the conditions for women's abuse.[3] It is also common for the lay leadership of the churches to consist disproportionately of the more successful members of the congregation: the more educated, prosperous, respectable members of the church community tend to be its public representatives. Thus the tendency of many to leave, or drift away from the church when faced with family disasters such as divorce, incest, rape, sustained unemployment, bankruptcy, and public knowledge of drug or alcohol addiction, or criminal charges against family members: those involved no longer see themselves as compatible with the public face of the church. The very face of the church seems to ostracize them in their times of greatest need.

With regard to sexual abuse, it is important to understand that the extent of victimization, which the churches have directly and

indirectly supported, is incalculably greater than the statistics num-
bering the women and children who have been abused, for two reasons. Such numbers do not include the effects on others of knowing
that they are potential victims of sexual abuse. In addition, such numbers do not include the many other forms of sexual victimization that
occur due to the fear of sexuality the churches have helped to perpetuate in our society.

What woman who, knowing the statistics on sexual abuse, deals
with the pain and suffering of a battered sister, neighbor, friend, or
daughter without feeling some level of fear when faced with the anger
of even a beloved spouse, much less the anger of other men less
known and loved? What woman who accompanies a friend through
the weeks and months of agonizing recovery from rape does not fear
to enter an empty house, go out alone, or otherwise enter a similar
situation that so afflicted her friend? The knowledge that there are
indeed innocent women and children all around us, some of whom
we know well, who are abused, often by someone they love, someone
we had learned to know and trust, cannot fail to lower our level
of trust toward others, especially men, who are the overwhelming
majority of sexual offenders.

Churches are supposed to preach love and trust of one another.
The failure of our churches to deal with sexual abuse means that not
only are men not directly discouraged from abuse of women and children, that the structures of patriarchal power that support such abuse
are not challenged, but most grievously, that some of the most serious
obstacles to love and trust among men and women are never touched
upon. How powerful can a message of love and trust be when it never
addresses principal obstacles to that love and trust?

In the aftermath of sexual violence, love and trust are broken, if not
destroyed both for victims and for all those who see themselves as
potential victims. The churches claim to be about reconciliation. But
reconcilation requires more than preaching that we must love and
trust one another. True reconciliation between victims and abusers is
rare, and often impossible. For true reconciliation requires first of all
repentance of the abuser. When the victim is convinced of the contrition of the abuser, the victim can then forgive, and full healing of
both is at least possible. These conditions are seldom satisfied. But
there is another level to reconciliation; it is a second best, but it is
the principal level to which the churches need to address themselves.
After sexual abuse both victims and those who see themselves as

potential victims feel unsafe; they see the world as dangerous, and no one in whom to trust. These victims and potential victims need to be reconciled to the world, to come to trust at least some persons. There may well be no completely safe places in the world, but victims have to relearn that there are some persons they can trust—that some people, men as well as women, love and respect them. In this task the churches can play an important role. The churches are limited in terms of pursuing full reconciliation: they do not have the resources, the ability, or the authority to locate, restrain, and bring to contrition all the abusers in the world. But they do have the ability to come before victims and potential victims and break company with victimizers. They can acknowledge the legitimacy of the fear of victims and potential victims, the fact that the world is not a just place, and that the innocent are victimized. The churches must affirm the innocence of victims to victims; this is the first step in breaking company with abusers and in restoring the capacity of victims to trust. It is especially important in view of the masculine face of church authority, for if victims and potential victims of sexual abuse by men are to see men and anything masculine as worthy of trust, they need support from men and masculine authorities such as the church.

OTHER FORMS OF SEXUAL VICTIMIZATION

One of the reasons why the responsibility of the churches for sexual victimization extends beyond the statistics on abuse is that there are many forms of victimization apart from physical sexual abuse. The churches are responsible to a large extent for the very understanding of sexuality which pervades our society, an understanding which is extremely deficient, and causes untold pain and suffering in a variety of ways aside from sexual abuse.

The churches know they are in trouble on sexuality, that there is a crisis of public confidence in the churches around the issue of sexuality, with different groups pulling the churches toward very different responses to that crisis. But there is no consensus in the churches on how to resolve the crisis over sexuality.[4] Some urge the churches to respond by reaffirming traditional teachings on sexuality; they argue that questioning traditional teachings and attempting to adjust them to modernity has created and continued to deepen the crisis. Others urge even fuller reform of church teachings on sexuality before the churches completely lose whatever of their credibility remains regarding sexuality; they insist that the roots of the crisis lie in the inconsistencies created in contemporary church messages on sexuality by an incomplete reform of traditional teaching.

I want to suggest that the properly Christian approach to the crisis over sexuality is a commitment to ending victimization, not to any purity of doctrine, whether purity be understood in terms of fidelity to the past or as consistency of reforms. Anyone who works in the area of sexuality knows what a wasteland it is—a waste of lives and relationships, a land of useless suffering. Some suffering cannot be avoided in human life, but the tragedy of human sexuality is that so much of the suffering in our sexual lives could be avoided. The churches bear greater responsibility for suffering in the area of sexuality than in many other areas because the church's influence on sexuality has been greater than in other areas of life.

What kinds of sexual victims are there besides victims of sexual abuse by others? Many. There are millions of persons who have suffered from and continue to suffer from sexual ignorance. There are adolescents who still don't know basic facts about pregnancy. Within the last five years I have taught sex education classes to 5th through 8th-graders in which sexually-active girls assured me that they can't get pregnant because they never have sex during their periods. Others believed that withdrawal was a foolproof contraceptive device; a few girls thought pregnancy resulted from French kissing, and one believed you have to want babies before you get pregnant (her mother's assurance). One girl who had recently reached menarche got hysterical with relief when she realized she wasn't dying, just having a period. A number of boys had been punished by parents for wet dreams—the parents insisted they had been masturbating. In working with adults I have also encountered otherwise ordinary persons who believe that sexual interest after middle age (female menopause) is perverse, and some who insist that the missionary position is the only moral option for marital intercourse; other positions are for immoral liaisons. All these people are victims of a sexual ignorance with the potential to deform their lives and relationships and those of their children to greater or lesser degrees.

SEXUAL IGNORANCE

Sexual Dysfunction

The most common forms of sexual dysfunction are those caused by ignorance. The failure to understand the role of vaginal lubrication in intercourse, and how to stimulate lubrication so that coitus is not painful for women, is responsible for sexual dysfunction in hundreds of thousands of women in our society. The failure to know that orgasm is possible, natural, and desirable for women is a major cause of anorgasmia, as is the failure of both men and women to understand that the majority of women require direct or indirect stimulation of the clitoris to reach orgasm; penile-vaginal intercourse provides sufficient stimulation for only about 30–44 percent.[5] Perhaps anorgasmia and painful sex do not seem major causes of suffering in themselves. But within marriage, anorgasmia and painful sex can be festering sores, the source of self-doubt and guilt, as well as of accusation. For anorgasmia is not merely the absence of female orgasm, and painful sex is not like a painful headache. Both are the absence of that which is right and natural, desired and expected by most partners in intimate sexual relationships—mutually pleasurable sexual communion, which is the source of one important kind of bonding, trust, and communication. Like involuntary infertility, anorgasmia and painful intercourse can wreck relationships. But unlike involuntary infertility, there are no legions of helpful experts to be found in the telephone book. Anorgasmia and painful sex are usually treated as a secret between the couple, thus lowering even further the chances of obtaining help. The churches are one important reason for the silence and secrecy around sexuality.

Lack of ejaculatory control in men (usually called premature ejaculation) is another common sexual dysfunction which wrecks relationships. It, too, is usually easily treatable by the couple themselves once the couple breaks through the secrecy and silence that surrounds sexuality and finds some accurate information.[6]

Homosexuality/Homophobia

Nowhere is sexual ignorance more evident than in popular attitudes toward homosexuality. Homophobia is rampant in our society, fueling an oppressive cycle of repression in which knowledge of homosexuality is itself understood as morally dangerous. Homophobia is regarded by many experts as responsible for the long delay in facing the AIDS crisis in the United States, and for continuing discrimination against individuals with AIDS in housing, employment, schools, and medical treatment. The all-too-popular assumption that AIDS is God's punishment for homosexuality clearly draws on the churches' longstanding condemnation of homosexual acts as immoral, for no one suggests that hemophiliacs dying of AIDS are being punished for hemophilia, or, in central Africa where the AIDS deaths are almost exclusively the result of heterosexual infection, that AIDS is punishment for being heterosexually active.

The churches have a moral obligation to inform their membership about homosexuality. Homosexuality is fundamentally an orientation—a sexual attraction to persons of the same sex. Sexual orientation is complex; many persons are not exclusively either heterosexual or homosexual, but only predominantly one or the other, with some attraction within the other orientation.[7] Persons act out their orientation in sexual behavior. Research indicates that the majority of persons who engage in homosexual acts, act out a predominantly or exclusively homosexual orientation that they did not choose, but only discovered in themselves, an orientation they often resisted and resented because of the intense social hostility to homosexuals. Sexual orientation, so far as we know, is fixed in most persons early in life, often before the person is sexually active, or even understands the significance of his or her attraction to others.[8]

We know that persons with homosexual orientation are even slightly less likely than heterosexuals to abuse or seduce the young.[9] We know that homosexual partnerships can demonstrate the same qualities of care, respect, and affection as committed heterosexual partnerships (marriages).[10] If the AIDS crisis has done nothing else positive, it has revealed to much of the general public the capacity of homosexual lovers for extended self-sacrificial love for sick and dying partners, as well as their capacity for forgiving each other for being the means, however unintentional, of contracting the disease.

How is it that the churches can overlook such evidence? There are at least three major reasons. The first is the popular perception of both psychological dysfunction and promiscuity among homosexuals. It is true that research indicates higher rates of psychological disturbance among homosexuals than heterosexuals. But we cannot assume that this higher rate is due to homosexuality itself. Any personal characteristic that evokes public disapproval, much less the estrangement from family, friends, employers, and neighbors that results from revealing one's homosexuality will frequently cause dysfunction. Exclusion, isolation, and derision do not produce healthy persons, but rather self-hatred. Until we can separate the effects of homosexuality from the effects of homophobia, we cannot label homosexuality dysfunctional, especially when we know that those homosexuals who value their homosexual orientation as intrinsic to their personhood demonstrate behavior and attitudes which are as healthy and well-adjusted as that of heterosexuals comfortable with their own orientation.[11] But society has made it much more difficult for homosexuals than for heterosexuals to achieve this sense of self-respect.[12]

The general public also tends to understand homosexuality in terms of unrestricted promiscuity, which is sometimes labeled the "homosexual lifestyle." As with most stereotypes, this label contains a grain of truth that cannot be legitimately universalized. Some part of the homosexual community is promiscuous (as is true of the heterosexual community). Before the AIDS epidemic forced a retreat from dangerous casual sex, about a quarter of male homosexuals were routinely engaging in frequent casual sexual encounters. About 10 percent were involved in monogamous relationships, another 18 percent in primary relationships along with some casual sexual encounters, and another sixteen percent were basically uninterested in sex and socially isolated.[13] Lesbians, however, tend to be more often engaged in monogamous relationships, and to have many fewer sexual partners over a lifetime.[14] In evaluating such statistics, we need to remember to compare them with the real behavior of heterosexuals, and not with some imagined ideal. In our society, half of all marriages end in divorce, usually followed by remarriage.[15] Rates of adultery in the United States stand at fifty percent for men, and approach fifty percent for women.[16] In the general population, sixty-eight percent of women and seventy-eight percent of men under the age of 19 have nonmarital sexual experience.[17] Homosexuals are not alone in high rates of multiple sex partners.

In addition, it is often pointed out that the rate of casual sex among heterosexuals falls in between higher rates of casual sex among homosexual males and lower rates of casual sex for homosexual women. It has been suggested that the lower rates for homosexual women, in conjunction with the historically lower (though rising) rates of nonmarital sex for heterosexual women indicate that social conditioning for men and women affect rates of promiscuity. Females are demonstrably more likely to connect sex and love, and to demand love and commitment before sex. Thus it makes sense that we find that male/male sex is the most casual, male-female sex a compromise between male and female conditioning, and female-female sex the most connected to love commitments. If this is so, then promiscuity among gay males is not so much due to homosexuality as it is to male social conditioning—a conditioning in which the churches have a role. To the extent that the sexual double standard is alive and well in the churches, the churches are complicit in the high rates of male homosexual promiscuity recorded before the AIDS epidemic.

A second reason that the churches have ignored research on homosexuality and maintained traditional condemnations is the belief that homosexuality is unnatural. The historic basis of this condemnation was the understanding that natural sex was procreative. The argument was that God created male and female sexuality in order to people the earth. But any church that has accepted the use of artificial contraception has severed any necessary link between sex and procreation. The basis for the churches' acceptance of contraception was the recognition that the primary, though not the only important purpose of sex is the intimate bonding created between the partners through mutual sexual pleasure. Children are a result of this bond; however, they are neither necessary for the bond, nor the purpose of the bond.

There are attempts to retain the argument that same-sex sexual activity is unnatural, apart from its non-procreative character. Those attempts focus on an interpretation of sexual differences between men and women as complementary. That is, human qualities are divided between men and women; to be whole, individuals must be bonded with a person of the other sex. Sexual complementarity characterizes historic understandings of sexuality; it is where we get the term "the opposite sex." The problem is that men and women are not opposites. There is no behavioral trait that is distinctively male or female. Most behavioral differences are clearly socially conditioned; those few differences that seem genetically or hormonally conditioned (for example, manual dexterity) are still not the exclusive property of one or the other sex.[18] Thus we have no assurance that among the people we encounter in a lifetime that the person who exhibits the most traits unlike our own will be someone of the other sex. We are beginning to uncover new anatomical/developmental differences between the sexes, for example, in brain research.[19] But we have no evidence thus far that these differences are absolute by sex (some women demonstrate the general male pattern, and vice versa), and such differences are not yet clearly linked to personality and behavior.

The attempt to emphasize sexual complementarity not only fuels victimization of homosexuals as unnatural persons, but also victimizes single people in our society, who are understood as being incomplete. The churches have no theological need for sexual complementarity. The second Genesis creation story (Gen. 2:4b–25), which is usually interpreted as the basis for sexual complementarity, is better understood as grounding social complementarity. We are social persons; our individual human personalities grow and develop through associations with others. For this reason, Adam was incomplete without Eve, for until Eve was created, he was alone, without human companionship. It was his human relationship with Eve, and not merely their sexual relationship, that offered opportunities for humaneness. We have opportunities for relationships with many different persons, males and females. We grow and change within these relationships, regardless of whether we are genitally intimate. To restrict our relationships to persons of either sex usually limits us, if only because every society generally and incompletely conditions the sexes to some specific differences, though these conditioned differences vary from society to society. We can all be whole and complete without sexual commitment to any other person, homosexual or heterosexual. The intimate bonding within sexual partnership is only one type among many types of intimate bonding.

A third reason for the churches' ongoing condemnation of homosexuality which blinds them to contemporary research data is grounded in the connection between homophobia and misogyny. To the extent that sexuality has been understood as basically heterosexual, it has been understood as involving a male and a female role. Within sexual activity itself, those roles have been understood in sexist ways: the male role has been understood as superior, active, and controlling, and the female role as inferior, passive, and controlled. Whatever dignity resided in the female role was invested in the reproductive function. From this perspective, male homosexuality is regarded as degrading to men, because it puts some men in the inferior female role, thus undermining the male claim to superiority and control.

Due to the influence of this perspective, many persons fail to appreciate that both male and female homosexuality, especially among the young, are much more free of dichotomous sex roles than is heterosexuality. Homosexual partners relate more as equal partners who share active and passive roles as well as control. For example, anal sex, which is often mistakenly assumed to be typical male homosexual activity because it is the closest analogy to heterosexual coitus, is actually practiced by only about a quarter of male homosexuals, and even then is not always practiced with consistent insertee/insertor roles. Such misunderstandings of roles in many of the cultures and subcultures which condemn homosexuality lead to attitudes of much greater disgust and censure for those homosexuals viewed as feminine and subordinant than for those viewed as macho and dominant, even when that dominant behavior entails violent coercion.

Thus the men who hold the majority of power in our churches often feel threatened by homosexuality. It represents both an abstract threat to male superiority, as well as the possibility that individual males could become sexual objects to other, more powerful, males. James Nelson suggests that another aspect of male homophobia is male envy of the male/male intimacy possible between male lovers, an intimacy which is both difficult to achieve in our society, even between fathers and sons, brothers, and friends, at the same time that it is desired and feared.[20]

If the churches understood homophobia as akin to racism, sexism, and prejudice against other ethnic or religious groups, they could be one source of accurate information about homosexuality, one force working toward reconciliation between homosexuals and homophobics, and a more effective voice for the message that God loves each and every one of us.

SEXUAL ATTITUDES

In addition to ignorance of basic sexual information, attitudes toward sexual activity can cause victimization. Doctors, ministers, counselors, and those who, like me, teach sexuality in churches and universities, still encounter women, and occasionally men, who were taught that sex is dirty and degrading, a threat to their virtue and only to be tolerated in marriage.[21] The social conditioning that teaches young women to be the gatekeepers—the dating partner whose role is to stay alert, to say no to sex—makes openness to and enjoyment of marital sex very difficult, for once married these women cannot easily tune out the old messages about lust and exploitation, dirt and disgust. Husbands often interpret this resistance to sex as evidence of lack of love and trust on the part of wives. Both husbands and wives become victims of such fear of sex.

For men, the teachings of the churches on male headship and responsibility for women in marriage pressure men to accept total responsibility for marital sex—not only for his pleasure, but for hers as well. Ignorance about sex, compounded by the resounding silence in the churches and in society about sex, creates an atmosphere devoid of support for sexual communication, which makes the man's task even more impossible. How can he know what she likes, unless he can ask and she feels comfortable enough to respond? Many women, knowing that men feel such responsibility for the female's pleasure, feel obliged to fake orgasm. Studies show that about two thirds of all women sometimes fake orgasm in order to make their partner feel he has fulfilled his responsibility to her.[22] There are a number of reasons why women fake orgasm, including inability to communicate to her partner what stimulation she requires, ignorance as to ways she could be orgasmic, or a desire to end intercourse due to fatigue or illness she did not feel free to communicate in the beginning. Faking orgasm further victimizes both men and women: women come to resent orgasmic deprivation, while men have no reason not to stick to methods of arousal which seem to have worked for their partner in the past, and thus have no clue as to their partner's resentment. Both are victims of their socially cultivated inability to communicate around issues of sexuality.

Masturbation is still considered morally objectionable by many persons, even though we know that self-stimulation of the genitals is instinctual in infants, and that infants as young as four months have been observed masturbating to orgasm[23]—long before they are capable of choosing to sin. We know that masturbation is often important in teaching people, especially women, their personal arousal patterns, knowledge that can greatly aid in the communication necessary for a satisfying sexual experience with a partner.[24] Furthermore, it is clear that the social stigma placed on masturbation despite the fact that virtually all males, and the overwhelming majority of females, masturbate, results in a furtiveness and secretiveness that teaches the young to obtain masturbatory gratification quickly and silently, lest they be caught. Unfortunately, this furtive haste often carries over to later partnered sexual activity and causes dysfunctions which interfere with sexual intimacy.

Why are people so ignorant about how their bodies work and unable to communicate about sexuality? Given the fact that over half of all couples experience one or more of the common dysfunctions, why is there so little help available, and so little effort to find help? The churches play a variety of roles in discouraging knowledge of sexuality. My own Catholic church insists on a multistep process of preparation for couples who are to marry in the church. That preparation usually (depending upon the diocese) includes some testing for maturity, personality match and other readiness issues, instruction on the sacrament of matrimony, and some instruction and discussion of financial matters, church involvement, division of household work, careers, and parenting. Rarely, if ever, is sexuality discussed; when it is, it is either treated as valuable because procreative, or presented in abstract terms as contributing to marital intimacy and cohesion. There is no instruction on how to make love, or on common sexual problems. There is often greater specificity on how to use a joint checking account than on how to physically love one another or communicate about that love. This in a church which understands marriage as a sacrament, which gives grace, and sexual intercourse as the sacramental sign which both creates and expresses that grace-giving love![25] The failure to instruct even engaged couples in how to make love well conveys a message that sex is both unimportant and instinctive. Belief in instinctive expertise further victimizes those with dysfunctions by making them feel abnormal, deficient, and alone with their problem, none of which is true.

Fear of Sex
The reason for the failure to instruct even the engaged, not to mention adolescents and the already married, on basic sexuality is clear. Our society, and even more strongly our churches, have not rid themselves of a fear of sexuality. Many observers of contemporary society laugh at the idea that our society fears sexuality—do we not see sex plastered all over magazines, billboards, movies, and TV? Where is fear of sex in a society in which half of all marriages involve sexual infidelity? In which we have the highest rate of illegitimate teen motherhood in the developed world?

And yet the fear of sexuality is at the root of these phenomena, too. There is a power in sexuality, a power that lies in its very attraction, its pleasure, its potential for satisfying our needs for bonding and intimacy. We have tried in much of the past Christian tradition to subdue the power of sexuality, to define it as dangerous, as rooted in a flesh prone to sin, as acceptable only when confined to marital intercourse for procreation. Christianity spent centuries urging either virginity over marital indulgence in sexuality, or, as second best, marital intercourse as untarnished by desire, lust or immoderate pleasure, and aimed at procreation. Frequently pastors have urged spouses to abstain from sex for a time in favor of prayer, lest too frequent sexual indulgence allow the devil to get his talons in us. Part of what we see in our society today is rebellion against this fear of sex, this separation of flesh and spirit in which sex represents the baseness of the flesh that threatens the divine spirit in us. But the forces of repression have become intertwined with the ultimately irrepressible human desire to embrace the power of our sexuality in many of our sexual attitudes and practices; the forces opposing repression have too often been distorted by that which they oppose.

Conflicting Attitudes and Practices
People cannot but be confused about sexuality, so conflicting are the various attitudes and practices confronting them. Some parts of

our society, especially those influenced by conservative Christian churches, still understand sex as dirty, sexual desire as dangerous, sexual ignorance as virtuous, and even marital sexuality as something hidden, not to be discussed, and basically motivated by procreation. This attitude forces a repression of sexuality. A competing social message is that sexuality entails a physical appetite like any other, that sex is natural, and that it is not healthy to abstain. This secular message assumes that all healthy, well-rounded human animals use sexual experimentation as a vehicle for finding a compatible mate. Another romantic version of the pro-sex message is that marital sexual love embodies divine love, and thus provides all one's personal needs: intimacy, passion, companionship, security, stimulation. Interestingly, all three of these attitudes can be found within the churches, though the second, that sex is a natural appetite, is not so much advocated as it is confirmed in the churches' blessing of those who located their partners for marriage through sexual experimentation. None of these understandings of sexuality are adequate.

Repression. The traditional Christian repression of sexuality recognized the power of sexuality but not the positive potential and even glory of sexuality in creating complex individuals and supporting Christian life. Sexuality cannot be repressed because it is not merely a category of actions but a dimension of persons. Every human action, to a greater or lesser degree, is sexual, because it is performed by sexual persons. Thus in some areas of our lives it becomes difficult to draw the line between what is sexual and what isn't. At one level, all of our actions are sexual because we are. But that does not mean that all of our actions lead to, or even suggest, genital sexual behavior. A casual hug and kiss between child and parent, two friends or two spouses may not only appear the same, but feel the same. Sometimes a backrub between lovers leads to arousal, and sometimes it doesn't. The same backrub between two friends may or may not produce physical arousal. For human beings, feelings are complex, and the line between what we call sensuality and sexuality resides not so much in what stimuli affect us, or even what physical feelings we experience from those stimuli, as in how we interpret those feelings and act on them. At the same time, the repressive approach to sex ignores the experience of glory possible in sexual communion, the experience of feeling at one, not only with one's partner, but with divine infinity itself. This potential for glory should not be surprising, for sexual intercourse in loving relationships has the potential for being a school for love—the same self-giving love which characterizes God.[26] In sexual intercourse the pleasurable experience of orgasm rewards us for the vulnerability, the letting go of control, of self-consciousness which makes orgasm possible. This experience can encourage us to become open and vulnerable to the other in nonsexual areas of the relationship, to give ourselves freely in the knowledge that we need not consciously pursue our own self-interest or the satisfaction of our own needs, because opening to the other who loves us also ensures our well-being. Such lessons in self-giving and trust can spill over into other relationships as well. Such is the essence of Christian life and of the gospel message of the realm of God.

Sex As Physical Appetite. The inadequacy of the secular message that sex is a natural appetite avoids the repression of the tradition but at the cost of not recognizing the power of sexuality. It is as if it says to the tradition that we need not fear sex, for sex is as ordinary as eating, and not dangerous or powerful at all. But sex is not really analogous to eating. This message fails to understand that sexuality is more than sexual activity, that it influences who we are, who we become, as well as what we do. The comparison of our hunger for food with our hunger for sexual activity is not really apt. At a superficial level, in both eating and sexual activity we look for variation in experience, new tastes and feelings that stimulate our interest. We can satisfy this desire for variation in a number of ways. We can seek a healthy diet that is varied in types, textures, and tastes of food, or we can stuff ourselves with a variety of high fat, low nutrient, junk foods with different tastes and textures, just as we can seek either a variety of partners or variety of experience within a committed relationship with one partner. But our urge to variety, to stimulation, differs a great deal from individual to individual and can also be satisfied in other areas of our lives. Some persons with very challenging, stimulating interests in their work or other involvements can be very well satisfied with a high degree of sameness in both their diet and their sexual experience.

At a more important level, however, we do not need sex in order to live as we do food. The primary urge that we feel toward sexual activity is not aimed at securing our physical existence, but at satisfaction of our need for bonding and intimacy, our urge to meld with another, to be wholly accepted, to no longer be alone. The failure to recognize this deeper level of sexual hunger can prevent its very satisfaction; it can promote sex as a physical activity without the psychic investment necessary to make sex as satisfying as it can be. It is also important to note that while sex has the power to satisfy the deepest longings of our spirit, it is not the only way to satisfy these longings, but one of many, and therefore the assumption that healthy, fulfilled persons are sexually active is not necessarily true. We can satisfy our yearnings for both stimulation and intimate bonding in many other ways: through friendship, art, nature, and shared work, among others.

Romantic Approach. The romantic approach to sex, which is inherently marital, has come to be faddish in progressive corners of the mainline churches. It has some very positive advances over the previous two approaches. It does understand sexuality as having the power and positive potential for divine communion, for expanding and creating love between partners. But it is often marred by its over-compensation for the negative assessments of sexuality in our past religious and secular traditions. Too often it is overly romantic and sentimental. It suggests that sex is not only a privileged, but the exclusive, method for experiencing divine communion.[27] In addition, the exaltation of marital sex and the marital relationship often implies and sometimes insists that the marital relationship satisfies all the needs of individual spouses. This overly romantic image of spouses as a self-sufficient unit puts utterly unrealistic pressures on marriages, for no one person can satisfy all the intimacy needs, much less all the other needs, of any individual. Human beings are social creatures; in order to develop our charisms and to truly know ourselves, we need a multiplicity of involvements, and we need to have ourselves reflected back to us by a variety of other persons from a variety of perspectives. The idea that romantic sexual love is enough can cause us to interpret any dissatisfaction we feel in our lives as evidence of the inadequacy of our sexual relationship. In fact, sexual relationships are but one part of our lives. We are also workers, children of our parents, neighbors, parents, friends, and members of larger communities. Problems in these relationships and environments are not erased by the fact that we love and are loved by our sexual partners. When we expect that love to be enough, we overburden our sexual relationships. We ask more than they can deliver.[28]

Yet another problem with this romantic approach to marital sexuality is its failure to deal with sexuality outside marriage, to recognize that eroticism is not limited to marriage. The attempt to put marital sex on a pedestal is often unconsciously aimed at masking the failure of the churches to truly examine sexuality in general, based on a desire to maintain traditional Christian rules surrounding sexuality. But the traditional rules were developed in tandem with the very negative attitudes about sexuality that we seek to shed. To hold onto the traditional rules while exalting marital sex leads to some serious problems and inconsistencies. For it inevitably occurs to the unmarried that a marriage license and the repetition of marriage vows are not the conditions that allow genital sexual activity to express and create love, commitment, and divine communion between the partners. They intuitively understand that shared intimate physical touch bonds persons together in care and trust, and that there are different degrees of care and trust, one building on the other. The fact that young adolescents, divorced and widowed persons, and single adults may not have partners to whom they are ready to commit themselves for life does not convince all of them that they should forgo genital sex, which seems to be presented to them as the most accessible means of the intimate bonding and divine communion they yearn for, even if they may acknowledge that their recourse to genital sex will yield less than the ideal harvest of bonding and communion. The churches need to examine this argument and stop refusing to recognize it on the grounds that the rules prohibit nonmarital sex.[29] The basic question is whether the traditional ban on nonmarital sex is rooted in attempts to repress all forms of sexuality which undermined a particular past public order, or whether the ban serves today to protect persons from suffering. Until the churches decide to reconsider the traditional ban, it cannot have an effective voice in this debate over sexual behavior.

PLEASURE AND ETHICS

Reconstructing Christian attitudes toward sex will require dealing with the issue of pleasure. As we saw in chapter 4, popular Christianity has come to see the cross as the symbol of human life on earth, and thus to stress the need to suffer. Albert Plé, in his *Duty or Pleasure? A New Appraisal of Christian Ethics*,[30] urges Christians to return to earlier theological approaches to ethics that grounded ethical activity in inherent human desires to maximize pleasure and minimize pain. He traces the steps Christianity took beginning in the Middle Ages from grounding ethics in pleasure to grounding ethics in duty.

Most Christians seem to understand ethical activity as the fulfilling of Christian duty, and are suspicious of attempts to base ethics on pleasure. If asked why they are suspicious, those who are able to give reasons beyond the fact of their own indoctrination in the churches respond that human beings are not capable of rational evaluation of their desire for pleasure. Their examples are usually sexual. Seeking pleasure, they say, leads to adultery. We can point in vain to the majority of persons who resist adultery out of the realization that indulging this momentary impulse could cost them the long-term pleasure of their marriages, family unity, and the respect of their friends. The major barrier to the acceptance of a pleasure-based ethics is the conviction of many that pleasure, and especially sexual pleasure, crowds out rationality, so that responsible choices between different pleasures is impossible. Sexual pleasure is seen as irresistible, and therefore dangerous and to be repressed. For many this fear of sexual pleasure has been generalized to all pleasure, so that pleasure should be ignored as a guide to what is valuable. This sometimes leads many to the contrary position—that what causes the most pain is the most valuable.

We must assert from our sexual experience that we can control our sexual urges, that we are both sexual and rational. Sexual pleasure is broader, deeper, and more complex than immediate sexual gratification. Within the process of intimate sexual relationships we learn to control desire for immediate gratification not out of duty to the partner, or duty to some abstract rule, but out of desire to enhance mutual pleasure. Young people who masturbate for sexual gratification have no difficulty renouncing masturbation when presented with opportunities for the mutual pleasure of partner sex. Men and women renounce sex for a time after childbirth out of mutual concern that the new mother heal quickly, so that they can share mutual sexual pleasure on a permanent basis in the future. Young men learn not to ejaculate at first impulse, but to delay gratification out of desire to prolong their own pleasure, and to be pleasured by the pleasure of their partners.

Shared pleasure bonds us together, whether we speak of sexual pleasure, the celebration of births and marriages, the success of community initiatives, or the harvest festivals of agricultural peoples. The bonds of shared pleasure make us care for one another, and out of that care comes good behavior toward one another. If we recognized the moral importance of pleasure, we would pay more attention to it, and learn to do an even better job of distinguishing shallow pleasures from deeper ones, momentary pleasures from abiding ones, and thus would make better moral choices.

If we recognized sexual pleasure as a good, we could begin to validate pleasure in other areas of our lives. Work, for example, should be pleasurable. That does not mean there will not be sweat and toil, frustration and exhaustion. But work should be chosen by individuals, and structured by organizations and institutions, so that it is pleasurable and satisfying. It should give us challenges to overcome, opportunities for success and pride, and for developing our talents. Too often we expect work to be consistently painful, to diminish us, and therefore do not exercise care in choosing and structuring work for ourselves and for others. Too often we teach children that education is a painful duty, to be followed by the even more painful duty of work. Our civic involvements and church activities should not be duties we take up reluctantly, but chosen because they offer us opportunity for pleasure: for contribution, leadership, community, and prideful achievement. These involvements will not always be easy, or convenient, but they should aim at pleasure. In these and many other areas of our lives we need to develop and trust our pleasure-seeking instincts.

SEX EDUCATION

In the debate over sex education in this nation, conservatives—and conservative churches—attempt to root out or water down sex education in the public schools. While religious liberals vehemently oppose such attempts, they themselves show little interest in the content of sex education in the schools other than an insistence on including contraception in the curriculum in an attempt to halt adolescent pregnancies. Most liberal churches hardly address sex education at all. Most Americans understand sex education as simply an explanation of reproduction beginning with female release of ova from the ovaries and male sperm production in the testes, moving through a mechanical description of penile release of semen in the vagina, followed by a description of conception and fetal development. The big question is understood to be whether contraception should be taught, and if so, whether methods of contraception are to be made accessible by the schools. But the real question about sex education is much broader: are we going to give our young information which allows them to cherish and feel comfortable with their own bodies, to physically express well their love to their sexual partners, to communicate well with their partners about sexuality, and to provide full information and models of sexual love to their own children? Information about reproduction is only the tip of the iceberg in adequate sex education.

Many school systems are now adding new sex education materials to the curriculum, materials designed to discourage sexual activity among youth. Young people should be taught how to say no to pressure for sexual activity they do not desire. But young people are not stupid. The message that they should say no to sex comes to them in a social context in which sexual experimentation offers them not only physical affection and intimacy, but also the only access to basic information about many physical, emotional, and relational aspects of sexuality. In a culture which not only glorifies sex in an abstract way as the answer to all intimate needs, but also masks the relational aspects of sex in a cloak of silence, it is no wonder that the message to "just say no" is so often regarded by young people as another instance of adults attempting to arbitrarily control their behavior. What is most necessary in sex education is to provide youth with full information on sexuality—on anatomical sex, techniques for both masturbation and shared sex, the physical and psychological processes of sexual maturation, sex and the aging process, and most importantly, personal perspectives on the meaning of sex and how it fits into human lifestyles. In order to do this well we need parents as well as teachers to break the silence about sexuality and speak about their experience of sex, what it means, and how it has changed throughout their lives. Research suggests that young people whose parents provided, or were a part of the provision of, full information and discussion of sexuality to their children are not more likely, and may be less likely, to experiment with sex early.[31] Youth who talk to their parents about sex, including contraception, are demonstrably more likely to use contraception if they are sexually active.[32] Even if broad sexual education did not discourage early experimentation, full information, including some instruction on the value and meaning of sex, is what we owe our children so that they can be responsible for their own lives as sexual persons.

If the churches' participation in restructuring the understanding of sexuality in our society is a moral obligation deriving in part from the churches' responsibility for past sexual repression, which continues to deform present attitudes, it still must be decided what is an appropriate role for the churches in such restructuring of attitudes. In light of the above, it seems to me that the churches should start with parents and other adults. The schools only really have access to the young; the churches have adults as well. Adult groups could either begin with discussion of sexuality, for example, sharing around marital sexuality, or sharing about parenting attitudes and practices around sexuality, or with bringing in persons who could share information.

Within preaching, adult Sunday school, and other more formal groups, perhaps the appropriate content with which to begin might be the doctrine of creation. Sexuality is an integral part of God's creation. Christians understand creation as good, as an expression of God's love. But it is clearly not enough to teach that sexuality is good because it is a part of God's good creation. Our tradition has too easily assumed that God's physical creation was created good, but was corrupted by human evil—that sexuality, in particular, has not only been corrupted by sin, but operates in the world as an instrument for further corruption. We must move beyond the general idea of sexuality as a created good.

God's self-expression in the history of the Judeo-Christian tradition—through scriptural revelation and revelation through the churches—does not replace God's communication through creation. Human beings experience God in all aspects of our lives, including sexuality. The very complexity of human sexuality can reveal to us the complexity of God, the difficulty in fully defining God, and the myriad sexual ways in which we can experience the presence of God. We can experience the divine presence in sexual intercourse, in the birthing of a child, in the hugs and kisses of our friends, in the discovery of new more effective methods of treating sexual dysfunction or sexually transmitted diseases, and in the awe-inspiring series of sexual changes which mark our individual physical maturation processes. But we will not always recognize the divine presence in these experiences unless the churches alert us to the possibility of such experiences of God.

CONCLUSION

The churches could learn something of God from many biologists and other scientists who explore creation. Many scientists are awed by the intricacy of the human body and all physical creation, and by the processes of evolution and development. They have a sense of participating in and probing the mystery of God through exploration and discovery of means for intervening in these processes as responsible co-creators with God, intent on using their understanding to both preserve creation and minimize human suffering. Scientists are fallible human beings, and sometimes intervene precipitously and irresponsibly in creation, without adequately estimating the effects of their actions on humankind or nonhuman creation. But the interest in and awe toward God's creation which attracts them to science could tremendously help the churches appreciate creation, and in particular sexuality, as offering experiences of God.

This is the place to begin sex education, with an appreciation of sexuality, with an understanding of its complexity and variation. Once we understand it better from biological, behavioral, psychological, and relational perspectives, then we can begin to probe sexual behavior with a focus on morality, instead of trying to conform our knowledge of sexuality to the behavioral rules we inherit, which is what too many in the churches have been doing. This attempt to conform our knowledge to inherited religious rules about sex is the real cause of the sexual crisis in the churches. Knowledge of distant events and facts can be suppressed, at least for a time, but experiential knowledge, knowledge of our bodies, of our relationships, of pleasure, cannot be repressed without both conflict within persons and institutions, as well as victimization of the innocent.

If the churches developed a real appreciation of sexuality, and reflected that appreciation in preaching, counseling, religious education programs as well as in denominational policy, it could not only help to drastically reduce the numbers of sexual victims in our society but it could also free up tremendous amounts of energy and resources to deal with other obstacles to the promotion of the kingdom. For if we truly appreciated and explored sexuality, we could begin to see the connections between our sexual attitudes and other justice issues plaguing our world.

There is hardly a justice issue in our country which does not have a sexual dimension. If we look at poverty, for example, we cannot miss the fact that poverty is disproportionately the lot of women and children, and strongly affected by divorce, teenage pregnancy, and economic discrimination against women. The arms race, and aggressive military and foreign policy have often been linked to social conditioning around masculinity: male identity and security are taught as requiring power and control, competition and winning, with no room for vulnerability or compromise.[33] Our ecological crisis is not called the rape of the earth for nothing. The understanding that the earth, like women, exists to be used and transformed according to male wishes has been basic to the scientific and industrial revolution which structured our modern world.[34]

It is no accident that disproportionate numbers of males become alcohol and drug addicts, petty criminals, and abandon their families, especially within the lowest economic class devastated by the replacement of well-paid industrial jobs with minimum-wage service jobs. The religious and secular definition of men as workers with two linked roles in the family—material provision and headship—means that un- or underemployment undermines men's role in the family and destroys feelings of self-worth.[35] If we did not define men's familial role as the linked tasks of breadwinner and headship, we would not condition children to associate control of material resources with legitimate authority. How many of us have heard—or said—"So long as you live in my home and I pay your bills, you do as I say"? Is it any wonder that such families produce children who grow up either to defer to those with wealth, or to expect to control those who have less wealth?

How much more democratic would the world be if churches abandoned the patriarchal family model, and urged shared decision making in the family? So long as church and society insist or assume that power in the family must be invested in one person, we cannot expect larger social units to truly attempt shared decision making. "Father (or Mother) knows best" is all too easily translated into "The expert (president, mayor, doctor, scientist, general) knows best; who are you to question?"

In conclusion, we do not have to be Freudians to recognize that sexuality colors every aspect of our world, every structure and decision that we make individually and collectively. Sexuality is not a distraction from the work of liberating victims, but an integral part of that work, which needs to be taken seriously by the Christian.

NOTES

CHAPTER 1

1. See, for example, Ernesto Cardenal, *The Gospel in Solentiname I* (Maryknoll, N.Y.: Orbis Books, 1976), or Robert McAfee Brown, *Unexpected News: Reading the Bible with Third World Eyes* (Philadelphia: Westminster Press, 1984).

2. See, for example, John McNeill, *The Church and the Homosexual*, (Kansas City: Sheed, Andrews & McMeel, 1976) or more recently John Shelby Spong, *Living in Sin: A Bishop Rethinks Sexuality?* (San Francisco: Harper & Row, 1988) for excellent treatments of the issue of scriptural authority.

3. I am indebted to Sue Ivory, an elementary school teacher who headed the Liturgy of the Word Program for Children at my former parish, for teaching me to see this story from the perspective of children. She refused to teach it to her classes over strong objections to her decision.

4. See, for example, "Letter From a Battered Wife," in Del Martin, *Battered Wives* (San Francisco: Glide, 1976), 1–5.

5. René Girard, *Violence and the Sacred*, 1972, trans. Patrick Gregory (London: Johns Hopkins University Press, 1977).

6. René Girard, *Job: The Victim of His People*, 1985, trans. Yvonne Frecerro (Stanford: Stanford University Press, 1987).

7. Karl Marx, "Theses on Feuerbach," in *The Marx-Engels Reader*, ed. Robert C. Tucher (New York: W.W. Norton, 1972) no. 9, 109.

8. I recognize that research is uncovering the fact that many more male children are sexually abused, and are victims of incest, than had been thought in the past. Much of the following argument applies to these male children as well. Nevertheless, I restrict myself here to females, not only since the vast majority of incest victims are female, but because research on female victims is much more advanced.

9. B. Janoff-Bulman and Irene H. Freize, "A Theoretical Perspective for Understanding Reactions to Victimization," *Journal of Social Issues* 39 (2): 1–17.

10. Diana H. Russell, *The Secret Trauma: Incest in the Lives of Girls and Women* (New York: Basic Books, 1986), 85.

11. Ibid., 158–160.

12. Russell, 190.

13. Robert Crooks and Karla Baur, *Our Sexuality*, 3rd ed. (Indianapolis, Ind.: Benjamin Cummings, 1990), 738.

14. Russell, 10.

15. Ibid., 231–232.

16. Gustavo Gutiérrez, *We Drink From Our Own Wells* (Maryknoll, N.Y.: Orbis, 1984) includes many brief accounts, as well as general description. Also see, Cardenal, *The Gospel in Solentiname*.

17. See my "Liberation Theology's Use of Scripture: A Reply to Its First World Critics," *Interpretation* (January 1987): 5–18.

18. Hugo Echegaray, *The Practice of Jesus* (Maryknoll, N.Y.: Orbis Books, 1980), 24, 91.

19. See Elisabeth Schüssler Fiorenza's treatment of her title reference in the introduction to *In Memory of Her: A Feminist Reconstruction of Christian Origins* (New York: Crossroad, 1983), 13; also Marie Fortune's treatment of women in scripture in *Sexual Violence: The Unmentionable Sin* (New York: Pilgrim, 1983), 44–61.

20. Schüssler Fiorenza, *In Memory of Her*.

21. W. E. Hewitt, "Myths and Realities of Liberation Theology: The Case of Basic Christian Communities in Brazil," *The Politics of Latin American Liberation Theology: The Challenge to U.S. Policy* (Washington, D.C.: Washington Institute Press, 1988), 144–146.

22. Carlos Mesters, "The Bible in Christian Communities," *The Challenge of Basic Christian Communities*, ed. Sergio Torres and John Eagleson (Maryknoll, N.Y.: Orbis Books, 1982), 207.

23. For an extended treatment of this theme, see my "Liberation Theology's Use of Scripture."

CHAPTER 2

1. Richard L. Rubenstein writes: "the classical Jewish and Christian readings of Scripture tend to interpret large scale misfortunes as divine chastisement for sin. Lest I be misunderstood, I cite this tradition as an historican of religion; it is not a tradition to which I personally subscribe. For example, over the centuries both church and synagogue have regarded the negative vicissitudes of Israel's history as divine punishment for Israel's want of obedience to the divine covenant." See "Liberation Theology and the Crisis in Western Theology," *The Politics of Latin American Liberation Theology: The Challenge to U.S. Foreign Policy*, ed. Richard L. Rubenstein and John K. Roth (Washington, D.C.: Washington Institute Press, 1988), 77.

2. See Gustavo Gutiérrez, *On Job: God-Talk and the Suffering of the Innocent* (Maryknoll, N.Y.: Orbis Books, 1987).

3. "Who will have pity on you, O Jerusalem,/ or who will bemoan you?/ Who will turn aside/ to ask you about your welfare?/ You will have rejected me, says the LORD,/ you are going backward;/ so I have stretched out my hand against you and destroyed you" (Jer. 15:5–6b).

4. Hosea 10:13–15 presents militarism as the cancer in the land; Hosea 4:1–3 sees the absence of kindness as causing mourning in the land. See also Jeremiah 5:7–9, 2:33–37, and Isaiah 65:11–12.

5. Monica Hellwig, "Good News to the Poor: Do They Understand It Better?" *Tracing the Spirit: Communities, Social Action, and Theological Reflection*, ed. James E. Hug (New York: Paulist Press, 1983). Also Gustavo Gutiérrez, *A Theology of Liberation* (Maryknoll, N.Y.: Orbis Books, 1983).

6. See Julio de Santa Ana, *Good News to the Poor: The Challenge of the Poor in the History of the Church* (Maryknoll, N.Y.: Orbis Books, 1979), chapters 5, 6.

7. Ernst Troelsch, *The Social Teaching of the Christian Churches*, Vol. 1, 3rd ed. (London: George Allen & Unwin, 1950), 184.

8. This position frequently presents itself as representing Christian Realism today. Reinhold Niebuhr is often quoted to support such a view, but it is significant that it is his theory, especially in *Moral Man and Immoral Society* and *The Nature and Destiny of Man*, which support this view. Much of his specific *politics* ran in the opposite direction. For example, his writings on race were explicit that the effects of past injustice prevent equal legal opportunity from producing equal achievement.

9. This is true, though with some adaptations, for Reinhold Niebuhr, who tended to idealize private relations and be cynical of public relations. See my "Parenting, Mutual Love and Sacrifice," in *Women's Consciousness, Women's Conscience: A Reader in Feminist Ethics* (New York: Winston, 1985).

10. In fact, Joe Holland and Peter Henriot depict this as typical of the Catholic church during the modern liberal period of 1878–1960s. See *Social Analysis: Linking Faith and Justice*. (Maryknoll, N.Y.: Orbis Books, 1983), 75.

11. See Frances Fox Piven and Richard A. Cloward, *Poor People's Movements: Why They Succeed and How They Fail* (New York: Vintage Books, 1977).

12. Piven and Cloward, *Poor People's Movements*, especially chapter 2, "The Unemployed Worker's Movement," and chapter 5, "The Welfare Rights Movement."

13. Pope John Paul II, *Laborem Exercens* (September 1981); U.S. Catholic Bishops, *Economic Justice for All: Catholic Social Teaching and the U.S. Economy*, 1986; Philip Berryman, *Our Unfinished Business: The Bishops' Letters on Peace and the U.S. Economy* (New York: Pantheon, 1988), 84–85.

14. See the testimony of workers quoted in John Raines and Donna Day-Lower, *Modern Work and Human Meaning* (Philadelphia: Westminster, 1986).

15. Stanley Aronowitz, *False Promises: The Shaping of American Working Class Consciousness* (New York: McGraw-Hill, 1973).

16. Aronowitz, *False Promises*, 26–27. See also Berryman, *The Bishops' Letters*.

17. Crooks and Baur, *Our Sexuality*, 653.

18. Rubenstein, "Liberation Theology," 72.

19. Hellwig, "Good News to the Poor," 125; Gutiérrez, *A Theology of Liberation*, 299–302.

20. Hugo Assmann, "Statement by Hugo Assmann," *Theology in the Americas*, ed. Sergio Torres and John Eagleson (Maryknoll, N.Y.: Orbis Books, 1976), 300.

21. Peter J. Paris, *The Social Teaching of the Black Churches* (Philadelphia: Fortress Press, 1985), chapter 5.

22. Pivin and Cloward, *Poor People's Movements*, 11.

23. Katharine H. Baur, "Economic Insecurity: A Family Problem," 67; John A. Schiller, "Poverty, Income and Wealth Trends," 25; Wallace H. Spencer, "Political Power and Poverty Policy," 112, *The American Poor*, ed. John A. Schiller (Minneapolis, Minn.: Augsburg Press, 1982).

24. One sustaining cause of this lack of leadership is that dominant groups are so skillful at co-optation. The leaders of protest and dissent are offered jobs within the bureaucracies controlled by the powerful. (Piven and Cloward, *Poor People's Movements*, 326–330, also 257.)

CHAPTER 3

1. Antonio Gramsci, *Selections From the Prison Notebooks* (New York: International Publishers, 1971).

2. Beverly Wildung Harrison, "The Power of Anger in the Work of Love: An Ethic for Women and Other Strangers," *Making the Connections*, ed. Carol Robb (Boston: Beacon Press, 1985).

3. Michael Harrington, *The Politics at God's Funeral* (New York: Penguin, 1983), chapter 3.

4. Schüssler Fiorenza, *In Memory of Her*, chapter 4, and Hugo Echegaray, *Practice of Jesus*, chapters 1, 3, 4.

5. Julio Santa Ana, *Good News to the Poor: The Challenge of the Poor in the History of the Church* (Maryknoll, N.Y.: Orbis Books, 1979), chapters 2–5.

6. Schüssler Fiorenza, chapter 5–7; Santa Ana, *Good News to the Poor*, chapters 2–5.

7. Santa Ana, *Good News to the Poor*, chapters 2–4.

8. Ibid., chapter 5.

9. Schüssler Fiorenza, *In Memory of Her*, chapter 4; Echegaray, *Practice of Jesus*, 84.

10. See, for example, Constance Parvey, "The Theology and Leadership of Women in the New Testament," Rosemary Radford Ruether, "Misogynism and Virginal Feminism in the Fathers of the Church," and Eleanor Como McLaughlin, "Equality of Souls, Inequality of Sexes: Woman in Medieval Theology," *Religion and Sexism: Images of Woman in the Jewish and Christian Religions*, ed. Rosemary Radford Ruether (New York: Simon & Schuster, 1974), and Rosemary Radford Ruether, *New Woman, New Earth: Sexist Ideologies and Human Liberation* (New York: Seabury, 1975), chapter 1.

11. Harrison, "Effect of Industrialization on the Role of Women in Society," *Making the Connections*; Eli Zaretsky, Captialism, the Family and Personal Life (New York: Harper & Row, 1975); and Philippe Aries, *Centuries of Childhood: A Social History of Family Life* (New York: Random House, 1965).

12. And were justified in thinking this way—for example, see papal

explanations in Christine E. Gudorf, *Catholic Social Teaching on Liberation Themes* (Lanham, Md.: University Press of America, 1980), chapter 5.

13. This is still true for many women; stereotypic femininity exercises a strong pull, and rejection of women's double burden, and of the ethic of sacrifice, is very difficult.

14. One of the most prominent examples of this is the bifurcated image of woman as virgin/whore, discussed by innumerable feminist writers in various disciplines.

15. This was probably first described in Herbert Marcuse, *One-Dimensional Man* (Boston: Beacon Press, 1964) and more recently by, among many others, Gregory Baum in his *Religion and Alienation* (New York: Paulist Press, 1975).

16. Margaret Atwood, *The Handmaid's Tale* (New York: Fawcett, 1985).

17. Gustavo Gutiérrez, "Two Theological Perspectives: Liberation Theology and Progressivist Theology," *The Emergent Gospel*, ed. Sergio Torres and Virginia Fabella (Maryknoll, N.Y.: Orbis Books, 1978).

18. Hugo Assmann, "Statement by Hugo Assmann," *Theology in the Americas*, ed. Sergio Torres and John Eagleson (Maryknoll, N.Y.: Orbis, 1976), 300.

19. Penny Lernoux, *Cry of the People: The Struggle for Human Rights in Latin America—The Catholic Church in Conflict with U.S. Policy* (New York: Penguin, 1982).

20. Peter Mayer, *The Pacifist Conscience* (New York: Holt, Rinehart, & Winston, 1966) and Roland Bainton, *Christian Attitudes Toward War and Peace* (Nashville: Abingdon, 1960), chapter 10.

21. Bainton, *Christian Attitudes*, chapters 6–8.

22. Amnesty International, 322 8th Avenue, New York, NY 10001.

23. Jon Sobrino, *Christology at the Crossroads* (Maryknoll, N.Y.: Orbis Books, 1978), 179–204.

24. Tom Driver, *Christ in a Changing World: Toward an Ethical Christology* (New York: Crossroad, 1981); Paul Knitter, *No Other Name? A Critical Survey of Christian Attitudes Toward the World Religions* (Maryknoll, N.Y.: Orbis Books, 1985).

25. Catherine Keller, "Sin, Self, and Violence." Paper presented at the meeting of the National Women's Studies Association, Urbana, Illinois, 12 June 1986.

CHAPTER 4

1. Mary Judith Ress, "Peru, Sendero Guerrillas Pose Uncertain Threat," *Latinamerica Press* 17, no. 27 (18 July 1985): 1–2.

2. Rolando Ames, "On Peru's Future," *World Policy Journal* 5, no. 4 (Fall 1988): 775.

3. I received varieties of this response from Senators Christopher Dodd and John Glenn, and Representatives Willard Gradison and Thomas Luken in response to my own letters.

4. Francis Bouchey, Roger W. Fontaine, David C. Jordan, and Gordon Summer Jr., *Santa Fe II: A Strategy for Latin America in the 90s* (Washington, D.C.: Council for Inter-American Security, 1989).

5. Ibid., 11.
6. Ibid., 12–14.
7. Taylor Branch, *Parting the Waters: America During the King Years 1954–1963* (New York: Simon & Schuster, 1988).
8. Ibid., 429–430.
9. Ibid., 509, 717–719, 825.
10. Herbert Lee's widow, and Bob Moses himself, blamed the voter-rights project (Branch, *Parting the Waters*, 510–511).
11. Branch, *Parting the Waters*, 731–737.
12. Gustavo Gutiérrez, *We Drink From Our Own Wells* (Maryknoll, N.Y.: Orbis Books, 1984), chapter 2.
13. Segundo Galilea, *The Beatitudes: To Evangelize As Jesus Did*, trans. Robert R. Barr (Maryknoll, N.Y.: Orbis Books, 1987).
14. Vatican Congregation for the Doctrine of the Faith, "Instructions on Christian Freedom and Liberation" (1986), chapter 3, pt. 4, 57.
15. Alice Walker, *The Color Purple* (New York: Washington Square Press, 1982), 167.
16. See Branch, *Parting the Waters*.
17. Lernoux, *Cry of the People*.

CHAPTER 5

1. See Martin, *Battered Wives*, chapter 1; and Fortune, *Sexual Violence*, 121–123.
2. Marie Fortune, "The Transformation of Suffering," *Christianity, Patriarchy, and Abuse: A Feminist Critique*, ed. Joanne C. Brown and Carole R. Bohn (New York: Pilgrim, 1989); Beverly Wildung Harrison, "The Power of Anger in the Work of Love: Christian Ethics for Women and Other Strangers," *Making the Connections*, especially 3–21.
3. Acknowledged in a landmark first draft statement on domestic battering by the Quebec Assembly of Catholic Bishops, "Violence en Heritage? Reflexion sur Violence Conjugale" (November 1989), one of the few indications that the churches recognize domestic abuse as a significant problem, let alone one for which they should be responsible.
4. In June 1991 the Presbyterian General Assembly rejected the "Report on the Special Committee on Human Sexuality," a very controversial plan for addressing anti-sexual, misogynist, and homophobic traditions in the church. (*Presbyterians and Human Sexuality: 1991*, Presbyterian Church U.S.A., 100 Witherspoon St. Louisville, Ky. 40202.) In August 1991 the Evangelical Lutheran Church adopted a proposed social statement, *Abortion*, in which the writers reached agreement only recognizing as moral abortions in the cases of rape, incest, severe fetal abnormalities, and risk to the life of the mother. The statement was adopted. A Methodist document on homosexuality and ministry should be public soon.
5. Crooks and Baur, *Our Sexuality*, 563; Helen Singer Kaplan, *The New Sex Therapy* (New York: Quadrangle, 1974), 122–125.
6. Kaplan, *New Sex Therapy*, 300–302.
7. Alfred C. Kinsey et al., *Sexual Behavior in the Human Male* (Philadelphia: Saunders, 1948), 638.
8. Sol Gordon and Craig W. Snyder, *Better Sexual Health: Personal Issues*

in Human Sexuality, 2d ed. (Boston: Allyn & Bacon, 1989), 70; Alan Bell, Martin Weinberg, and Sue K. Hammersmith, *Sexual Preference: Its Development in Men and Women* (Bloomington, Ind.: Indiana University Press, 1981), 211.

9. Bell, Weinberg and Hammersmith, *Sexual Preference*, 222; Alan Bell and Martin Weinberg, *Homosexualities: A Study of Diversity Among Men and Women* (New York: Simon & Schuster, 1978), 230.

10. See Letitia A. Peplau's study reported in, "What Homosexuals Want in Relationships," *Psychology Today*, March 1981, 28–38.

11. Bell and Weinberg, *Homosexualities*, 216.

12. The tasks involved in achieving psychological health and spiritual well-being are not so much distinct for gays and straights as are the experiential obstacles involved, as is clear to any heterosexual reading John McNeill's excellent book, *Taking a Chance on God: Liberating Theology for Gays, Lesbians, and Their Lovers, Families, Friends* (Boston: Beacon Press, 1988).

13. Bell and Weinberg, *Homosexualities*, 217–228.

14. Barbara C. Leigh, "Reasons for Having and Avoiding Sex: Gender, Sexual Orientation, and Relationship to Sexual Behavior," *Journal of Sex Research* 26 (1989): 199–208.

15. Jean M. Lown and E. M. Dolan, "Financial Challenges in Remarriage," *Lifestyles: Family and Economic Issues* 9 (1988): 73–74.

16. Crooks and Baur, *Our Sexuality*, 513–515, for a survey of studies.

17. Melvin Zelnick and J. Kantner, "Sexual Activity, Contraceptive Use, and Pregnancy Among Metropolitan Area Teenagers," *Family Planning Perspectives* 12 (1980): 230–239.

18. Even the hormonal conditioning can be overridden by strong cultural pressure: see Margaret Mead's study of three Papua New Guinea tribes with regard to aggression, which has since been shown to be linked to androgen levels; Margaret Mead, *Sex and Temperament in Three Primitive Societies* (New York: Morrow, 1963).

19. F. Bloom, A. Lazerson, and L. Hofstadter, *Brain, Mind and Behavior* (New York: Freeman, 1985); R. Thompson, *The Brain* (New York: Freeman, 1985), 164.

20. James Nelson, *The Intimate Connection: Male Sexuality, Masculine Spirituality* (Philadelphia: Westminster Press, 1988), 62.

21. Charles Gallagher et al., *Embodied in Love* (New York: Crossroad, 1986), 65–67.

22. Crooks and Baur, *Our Sexuality*, 568–569. Men, too, sometimes fake orgasm, but only about half as often as women, usually to cover up what they regard as inadequate sexual performance.

23. Kinsey et al., *Sexual Behavior*, 177.

24. Eleanor Hamilton, *Sex, With Love* (Boston: Beacon Press, 1978), 33.

25. Gallagher et al., *Embodied in Love*, chapter 1.

26. Ibid.

27. This is the problem with Gallagher et al., *Embodied in Love* and other attempts to reclaim sexuality as spiritually relevant, as well as with much secular thinking on sexual love. While it is important to reclaim sexuality in general as an intrinsic part of human beings which mediates all of our social experience and therefore all of our experience of divine presence, genital

sexual activity is only one aspect of our sexuality. While it may well be in our society one of the most accessible and recognizable means for experiencing divine love, this is only partly the result of the inherent potential in genital sexual activity. It is also one result of the social predisposition to look for primary meaning, satisfaction and communion in genital sexual expression, a predisposition which is not true of all cultures.

28. For one explanation of how our society came to place such great burdens of meaning and satisfaction on private marital relationships, see Eli Zaretsky, *Capitalism, the Family and Personal Life* (New York: Harper & Row, 1976), chapters 3, 4.

29. See Episcopal Bishop John Shelby Spong's honest treatment of this issue in his *Living in Sin?*.

30. Albert Plé, O.P., *Duty or Pleasure? A New Appraisal of Christian Ethics*. Trans. Matthew J. O'Connell. (New York: Paragon, 1987).

31. Joyce L. Goldfarb et al., "An Attempt to Detect 'Pregnancy Susceptibility' in Indigent Adolescent Girls," *Journal of Youth and Adolescence* 6 (1977): 127–144; Graham B. Spanier, "Sources of Sex Information and Premarital Sexual Behavior," *Journal of Sex Research* 13 (1977): 73–88.

32. Sharon A. Baker et al., "Parents Behavioral Norms as Predictors of Adolescent Sexual Activity and Contraceptive Use," *Adolescence* 23 (1988): 278–281.

33. Marc Feigan Fasteau, *The Male Machine* (New York: McGraw-Hill, 1974), chapters 12, 13; Nelson, *The Intimate Connection*, chapters 3, 4.

34. Carolyn Merchant, *The Death of Nature: Women, Ecology and the Scientific Revolution* (San Francisco: Harper & Row, 1980).

35. Ruth Sidell, "Where Are the Men?" in *Women and Children Last* (New York: Penguin, 1986). The importance of the breadwinner role for masculine identity seems to be true not only of traditional concepts of masculinity, but also of the new directions of masculinity: Joseph H. Pleck, *The Myth of Masculinity* (Cambridge, Mass.: MIT Press, 1981), 151–152.

BIBLIOGRAPHY

Adriance, Madeleine. *Opting for the Poor: Brazilian Catholicism in Transition.* Kansas City: Sheed and Ward, 1986.

Ames, Roilando, "On Peru's Future." *World Policy Journal* 5:4 (Fall 1988), 775.

Andolsen, B., et al. *Women's Consciousness, Women's Conscience: A Reader in Feminist Ethics.* Minneapolis: Winston, 1985.

Aries, Phillippe. *Centuries of Childhood: A Social History of the Family.* New York: Random House, 1965.

Aronowitz, Stanley. *False Promises: The Shaping of American Working-Class Consciousness.* New York: McGraw-Hill, 1973.

Atwood, Margaret. *The Handmaid's Tale.* New York: Fawcett, 1985.

Bainton, Roland. *Christian Attitudes Toward War and Peace.* Nashville: Abingdon, 1960.

Baum, Gregory, and Robert Ellsberg, eds. *The Logic of Solidarity: Commentaries on Pope John Paul II's Encyclical "On Social Concern."* Maryknoll, N.Y.: Orbis, 1989.

_____. *Religion and Alienation.* New York: Paulist, 1975.

Bell, Alan, Martin Weinberg, and Sue Hammersmith. *Sexual Preference: Its Development in Men and Women.* Bloomington, Ind.: Indiana University Press, 1981.

Berryman, Philip. *Liberation Theology.* New York: Pantheon, 1987.

_____. *Our Unfinished Business: The Bishops' Letters on Peace and the Economy.* New York: Pantheon, 1989.

Bouchey, Francis, Roger W. Fontaine, David C. Jordan, and Gordon Summer, Jr. *Santa Fe II: A Strategy for Latin America in the 90's.* Washington, D.C.: Council for Inter-American Society, 1989.

Branch, Taylor. *Parting the Waters: America During the King Years 1954– 1963.* New York: Simon and Schuster, 1988.

Brown, Joanne C., and Carole R. Bohn, eds. *Christianity, Patriarchy, and Abuse: A Feminist Critique.* New York: Pilgrim, 1989.

Brown, Robert McAfee. *Unexpected News: Reading the Gospel with Third World Eyes.* Philadelphia: Westminster, 1984.

Cannon, Katie G. *Black Womanist Ethics.* Atlanta: Scholars Press, 1988.

Cardenal, Ernesto. *The Gospel in Solentiname.* Maryknoll, N.Y.: Orbis, 1976.

Chapman, Jane R., and Margaret Gates. *The Victimization of Women*. Beverly Hills, Calif.: Sage, 1978.

Crooks, Robert, and Karla Baur. *Our Sexuality*. Indianapolis: Benjamin Cummings, 1990.

Daly, Herman E., and John B. Cobb, Jr. *For the Common Good: Redirecting the Economy Toward Community, the Environment, and a Sustainable Future*. Boston: Beacon, 1989.

Driver, Tom. *Christ in A Changing World: Toward an Ethical Christology*. New York: Crossroad, 1981.

Dussel, Enrique. *Ethics and Community*. Trans. Robert R. Barr. Maryknoll, N.Y.: Orbis, 1988.

Echegaray, Hugo. *The Practice of Jesus*. Trans. Matthew J. O'Connell. Maryknoll, N.Y.: Orbis, 1984.

Feigan-Fasteau, Marc. *The Male Machine*. New York: McGraw-Hill, 1974.

Fortune, Marie. *Sexual Violence: The Unmentionable Sin*. New York: Pilgrim, 1983.

Galilea, Segundo. *The Beatitudes: To Evangelize As Jesus Did*. Trans. Robert R. Barr. Maryknoll, N.Y.: Orbis, 1987.

Gallagher, Charles, et al. *Embodied in Love: Sacramental Spirituality and Sexual Intimacy*. New York: Crossroad, 1986.

Girard, René. *Job: Victim of His People*. Trans. Yvonne Frecerro. Stanford, Calif.: Stanford University Press, 1977.

_____. *Violence and the Sacred*. Trans. Patrick Gregory. Stanford, Calif.: Stanford University Press, 1977.

Goldfarb, Joyce L., et al. "An Attempt to Detect 'Pregnancy Susceptibility' in Indigent Adolescent Girls." *Journal of Youth and Adolescence* 6 (1977): 127–44.

Gordon, Sol, and Craig W. Snyder. *Better Sexual Health: Personal Issues in Human Sexuality*. 2d ed. Boston: Allyn and Bacon, 1989.

Gramsci, Antonio. *Selections from Prison Notebooks*. Trans. and ed. Quintin Hoare and Geoffrey Nowell Smith. New York: International Publishers, 1971.

Gudorf, Christine E. *Catholic Social Teaching on Liberation Themes*. Lanham, Md.: University Press of America, 1980.

_____. "Liberation Theology's Use of Scripture: A Reply to Its First World Critics." *Interpretation* (January 1987): 5–18.

Gutiérrez, Gustavo. *On Job: God Talk and the Suffering of the Innocent*. Trans. Matthew J. O'Connell. Maryknoll, N.Y.: Orbis, 1987.

_____. *A Theology of Liberation*. Trans. and ed. Sr. Caridad Inda and John Eagleson. Maryknoll, N.Y.: Orbis, 1974.

_____. *We Drink From Our Own Wells: The Spiritual Journey of a People*. Trans. Matthew J. O'Connell. Maryknoll, N.Y.: Orbis, 1984.

Hamilton, Eleanor. *Sex, With Love*. Boston: Beacon, 1978.

Harrington, Michael. *The Politics at God's Funeral*. New York: Penguin, 1983.

Harrison, Beverly W. *Making the Connections: Essays in Feminist Social Ethics*. Intro. Carol S. Robb. Boston: Beacon, 1985.

_____, et al. *The Public Vocation of Ethics*. New York: Pilgrim, 1986.

Heyward, Carter. *Touching Our Strength: The Erotic as Power and the Love of God*. San Francisco: HarperCollins, 1989.

Holland, Joe, and Peter Henriot. *Social Analysis: Linking Faith and Justice*.

Maryknoll, N.Y.: Orbis, 1983.

Hooks, Bell. *Yearning: Race, Gender, and Cultural Politics*. Boston: South End Press, 1990.

Hug, James E. *Tracing the Spirit: Communities, Social Action, and Theological Reflection*. New York: Paulist, 1983.

Janoff-Bulman, B., and Irene H. Freize. "A Theoretical Perspective for Understanding Reactions to Victimization." *Journal of Social Issues* 39 (2): 1–17.

John Paul II. "Laborem Exercens." *Origins* 11:15 (Sept. 24, 1981).

Kaplan, Helen Singer. *The New Sex Therapy*. New York: Quadrangle, 1974.

Keller, Catharine. "Sin, Self, and Violence." Unpublished paper presented at National Women's Studies Association, Urbana, Ill., June 12, 1986.

Kinsey, Alfred C., et al. *Sexual Behavior in the Human Male*. Philadelphia: Saunders, 1948.

Knitter, Paul. *No Other Name? A Critical Survey of Christian Attitudes Toward the World Religions*. Maryknoll, N.Y.: Orbis, 1985.

Leigh, Barbara C. "Reasons for Having and Avoiding Sex: Gender, Sexual Orientation, and Relationship to Sexual Behavior." *Journal of Sex Research* 26 (1989): 199–208.

Lernoux, Penny. *Cry of the People: The Struggle for Human Rights in Latin America*. New York: Penguin, 1982.

————. *In Banks We Trust: Bankers and Their Close Associates (The CIA, the Mafia, Drug Traders, Dictators, Politicians, and the Vatican)*. Garden City, N.Y.: Doubleday, 1984.

Lown, Jean M., and E. M. Dolan. "Financial Challenges in Remarriage." *Lifestyles: Family and Economic Issues* 9 (1988): 73–74.

Marcuse, Herbert. *One Dimensional Man*. Boston: Beacon, 1964.

Martin, Del. *Battered Wives*. San Francisco: Glide, 1976.

McNeill, John. *The Church and the Homosexual*. Kansas City: Sheed, Andrews and McMeel, 1976.

————. *Taking a Chance on God: Liberating Theology for Gays, Lesbians, and Their Lovers, Families, Friends*. Boston: Beacon, 1988.

Mead, Margaret. *Sex and Temperament in Three Primitive Societies*. New York: Morrow, 1963.

Merchant, Carolyn. *The Death of Nature: Women, Ecology, and the Scientific Revolution*. San Francisco: Harper and Row, 1980.

Nelson, James B. *The Intimate Connection: Male Sexuality, Masculine Spirituality*. Philadelphia: Westminster, 1988.

Niebuhr, Reinhold. *Moral Man and Immoral Society*. New York: Charles Scribner's Sons, 1932, 1960.

————. *The Nature and Destiny of Man*. Comb. vols. 1 and 2. New York: Charles Scribner's Sons, 1941, 1964.

Paris, Peter. *The Social Teaching of the Black Churches*. Philadelphia: Fortress, 1985.

Peplau, Letitia A. "What Homosexuals Want in Relationships." *Psychology Today* (March 1981): 28–38.

Piven, Frances Fox, and Richard A. Cloward. *Poor People's Movements: Why They Succeed and How They Fail*. New York: Vintage, 1977.

Plé, Albert. *Duty or Pleasure? A New Appraisal of Christian Ethics*. Trans. Matthew J. O'Connell. New York: Paragon, 1987.

Pleck, Joseph H. *The Myth of Masculinity.* Cambridge: MIT Press, 1981.

Quebeck Assembly of Catholic Bishops (Social Action Committee). *Violence en Heritage? Reflexion sur Violence Conjugale.* Montreal: Quebec Assembly of Bishops, 1989.

Raines, John, and Donna Day-Lower. *Modern Work and Human Meaning.* Philadelphia: Westminster, 1986.

Ress, Mary Judith. "Peru, Sendero Guerrilas Pose Uncertain Threat." *Latinamerica Press* 17:27 (July 18, 1985): 1–2.

Rubenstein, Richard L., and John K. Roth, eds. *The Politics of Latin American Liberation Theology: The Challenge to U.S. Foreign Policy.* Washington, D.C.: Washington Institute Press, 1988.

Ruether, Rosemary R. *New Women, New Earth: Sexist Ideologies and Human Liberation.* New York: Seabury, 1975.

———. *Religion and Sexism: Images of Women in the Jewish and Christian Religions.* New York: Simon and Schuster, 1974.

Russell, Diana E. H. *The Secret Trauma: Incest in the Lives of Girls and Women.* New York: Basic, 1986.

Santa Ana, Julio de. *Good News to the Poor: The Challenge of the Poor in the History of the Church.* Trans. Helen Whittle. Maryknoll, N.Y.: Orbis, 1979.

Schiller, John A., ed. *The American Poor.* Minneapolis: Augsburg, 1982.

Schüssler Fiorenzsa, Elisabeth. *In Memory of Her: A Feminist Theological Reconstruction of Christian Origins.* New York: Crossroad, 1983.

Sidell, Ruth. *Women and Children Last.* New York: Penguin, 1986.

Spanier, Graham B. "Sources of Sex Information and Premarital Sexual Behavior." *Journal of Sex Research* 13 (1977): 73–88.

Special Committee on Human Sexuality. *Presbyterians and Human Sexuality: 1991.* Louisville: Westminster, 1991.

Sobrino, Jon. *Christology at the Crossroads.* Maryknoll, N.Y.: Orbis, 1978.

Spong, John Shelby. *Living in Sin? A Bishop Rethinks Human Sexuality.* San Francisco: Harper and Row, 1988.

Thistlethwaite, Susan. *Sex, Race, and God: Christian Feminism in Black and White.* New York: Crossroad, 1991.

Torres, Sergio, and John Eagleson, eds. *The Challenge of Basic Christian Communities.* Maryknoll, N.Y.: Orbis, 1982.

Troeltsch, Ernst. *The Social Teaching of the Christian Churches.* Vol. 1, 3d ed. London: George Allen and Unwin, 1950.

Tucker, Robert C., ed. *The Marx-Engels Reader.* New York: W. W. Norton, 1972.

Vatican Congregation for the Doctrine of the Faith. "Instructions on Certain Aspects of the Theology of Liberation." *National Catholic Reporter* (Sept. 21, 1984).

———. "Instructions on Christian Freedom and Liberation." *Origins* 15:44 (April 17, 1986): 714–27.

Walker, Alice. *The Color Purple.* New York: Washington Square Press, 1982.

Zaretsky, Eli. *Capitalism, the Family and Personal Life.* New York: Harper and Row, 1975.

Zelnick, Melvin, and J. Kanter. "Sexual Activity, Contraceptive Use, and Pregnancy Among Metropolitan Area Teenagers." *Family Planning Perspectives* 12 (1980): 230–239.